EXPLORING PLANET EARTH

Anthea Maton
Former NSTA National Coordinator
Project Scope, Sequence, Coordination
Washington, DC

Jean Hopkins
Science Instructor and Department Chairperson
John H. Wood Middle School
San Antonio, Texas

Susan Johnson
Professor of Biology
Ball State University
Muncie, Indiana

David LaHart
Senior Instructor
Florida Solar Energy Center
Cape Canaveral, Florida

Maryanna Quon Warner
Science Instructor
Del Dios Middle School
Escondido, California

Jill D. Wright
Professor of Science Education
Director of International Field Programs
University of Pittsburgh
Pittsburgh, Pennsylvania

Prentice Hall
Englewood Cliffs, New Jersey
Needham, Massachusetts

Prentice Hall Science

Exploring Planet Earth

Student Text and Annotated Teacher's Edition
Laboratory Manual
Teacher's Resource Package
Teacher's Desk Reference
Computer Test Bank
Teaching Transparencies
Product Testing Activities
Computer Courseware
Video and Interactive Video

The illustration on the cover, rendered by Keith Kasnot, shows a research satellite in Earth's orbit.

Credits begin on page 184.

SECOND EDITION

ISBN 0-13-400599-6

6 7 8 9 10   97 96 95 94

Prentice Hall
A Division of Simon & Schuster
Englewood Cliffs, New Jersey 07632

STAFF CREDITS

Editorial:	Harry Bakalian, Pamela E. Hirschfeld, Maureen Grassi, Robert P. Letendre, Elisa Mui Eiger, Lorraine Smith-Phelan, Christine A. Caputo
Design:	AnnMarie Roselli, Carmela Pereira, Susan Walrath, Leslie Osher, Art Soares
Production:	Suse F. Bell, Joan McCulley, Elizabeth Torjussen, Christina Burghard
Photo Research:	Libby Forsyth, Emily Rose, Martha Conway
Publishing Technology:	Andrew Grey Bommarito, Deborah Jones, Monduane Harris, Michael Colucci, Gregory Myers, Cleasta Wilburn
Marketing:	Andrew Socha, Victoria Willows
Pre-Press Production:	Laura Sanderson, Kathryn Dix, Denise Herckenrath
Manufacturing:	Rhett Conklin, Gertrude Szyferblatt

Consultants

Kathy French	National Science Consultant
Jeannie Dennard	National Science Consultant
Brenda Underwood	National Science Consultant
Janelle Conarton	National Science Consultant

CONTENTS

EXPLORING PLANET EARTH

SCIENCE GAZETTE

Activity Bank/Reference Section

Features

CONCEPT MAPPING

Throughout your study of science, you will learn a variety of terms, facts, figures, and concepts. Each new topic you encounter will provide its own collection of words and ideas—which, at times, you may think seem endless. But each of the ideas within a particular topic is related in some way to the others. No concept in science is isolated. Thus it will help you to understand the topic if you see the whole picture; that is, the interconnectedness of all the individual terms and ideas. This is a much more effective and satisfying way of learning than memorizing separate facts.

Actually, this should be a rather familiar process for you. Although you may not think about it in this way, you analyze many of the elements in your daily life by looking for relationships or connections. For example, when you look at a collection of flowers, you may divide them into groups: roses, carnations, and daisies. You may then associate colors with these flowers: red, pink, and white. The general topic is flowers. The subtopic is types of flowers. And the colors are specific terms that describe flowers. A topic makes more sense and is more easily understood if you understand how it is broken down into individual ideas and how these ideas are related to one another and to the entire topic.

It is often helpful to organize information visually so that you can see how it all fits together. One technique for describing related ideas is called a **concept map**. In a concept map, an idea is represented by a word or phrase enclosed in a box. There are several ideas in any concept map. A connection between two ideas is made with a line. A word or two that describes the connection is written on or near the line. The general topic is located at the top of the map. That topic is then broken down into subtopics, or more specific ideas, by branching lines. The most specific topics are located at the bottom of the map.

To construct a concept map, first identify the important ideas or key terms in the chapter or section. Do not try to include too much information. Use your judgment as to what is really important. Write the general topic at the top of your map. Let's use an example to help illustrate this process. Suppose you decide that the key terms in a section you are reading are School, Living Things, Language Arts, Subtraction, Grammar, Mathematics, Experiments, Papers, Science, Addition, Novels. The general topic is School. Write and enclose this word in a box at the top of your map.

SCHOOL

Now choose the subtopics—Language Arts, Science, Mathematics. Figure out how they are related to the topic. Add these words to your map. Continue this procedure until you have included all the important ideas and terms. Then use lines to make the appropriate connections between ideas and terms. Don't forget to write a word or two on or near the connecting line to describe the nature of the connection.

Do not be concerned if you have to redraw your map (perhaps several times!) before you show all the important connections clearly. If, for example, you write papers for Science as well as for Language Arts, you may want to place these two subjects next to each other so that the lines do not overlap.

One more thing you should know about concept mapping: Concepts can be correctly mapped in many different ways. In fact, it is unlikely that any two people will draw identical concept maps for a complex topic. Thus there is no one correct concept map for any topic! Even though your concept map may not match those of your classmates, it will be correct as long as it shows the most important concepts and the clear relationships among them. Your concept map will also be correct if it has meaning to you and if it helps you understand the material you are reading. A concept map should be so clear that if some of the terms are erased, the missing terms could easily be filled in by following the logic of the concept map.

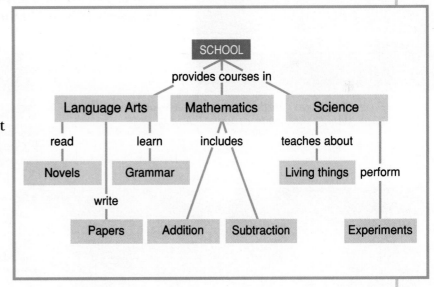

EXPLORING PLANET EARTH

As the *Voyager* spacecraft began its epic journey among the planets of the solar system, it sent back a portrait of the Earth and its moon. During its 13-year voyage, the sturdy spacecraft was to send back thousands of stunning images of the outer planets and their moons before disappearing into the depths of space. But of all the planets and moons on *Voyager*'s travels, Planet Earth is unique.

▲ *From the moon, Earth appears as a watery blue planet with swirls of white clouds.*

▲ *This photograph of clouds near the top of the Matterhorn in Switzerland illustrates two features of Earth—landmasses and an atmosphere. Of all the planets, only Earth contains liquid water.* ◄

Of all the planets in our solar system, only Earth has oceans and rivers of liquid water on its surface. And only Earth is surrounded by a blanket of breathable air. In the pages that follow, you will learn about the Earth's oceans, its freshwater lakes and rivers, and the atmosphere that surrounds it. You will also learn about Earth's landmasses—its mountains, plains, and plateaus. And you will take a journey to the center of the Earth to study its interior.

Voyager has given us a valuable glimpse of the worlds that make up the sun's family. In this textbook, you will explore the world that interests us most—our home, Planet Earth.

Raging Iguassu Falls in Brazil demonstrates how Earth's surface is changed by moving water.

Discovery *Activity*

Neighborhood Mapping

Use a large sheet of plain, white paper and colored pencils to draw a map of your neighborhood. Show the location of houses, schools, libraries, streets, and other local features, as well as any natural features such as bodies of water. Include a scale and a key to indicate direction on your neighborhood map.

■ Trade maps with a classmate. Can you find your way around using your classmate's map? Can your classmate use your map to find a specific location in your neighborhood?

■ What features make a map useful?

Earth's Atmosphere

People have walked on the surface of the moon. Machines have landed upon and scratched at the surface of Mars. Rockets have carried satellites on photographic missions into the darkness of space beyond the farthest reaches of our solar system. These voyages of exploration represent great leaps that took the minds—and sometimes even the bodies—of humans far from the comforts of their Earthly home.

Yet people forget that Earth too is a wondrous planet on a fantastic voyage. In just one year's time, Earth will make a complete trip around the sun—taking you, your family and friends, and the remainder of humanity on a fabulous journey. In many ways, Earth is like a giant spacecraft transporting a special cargo of life.

Why is Earth the only planet in our solar system uniquely able to support life? In this chapter you will learn about the Earth's atmosphere—the special envelope of air that surrounds our planet home as it journeys through space. The atmosphere is one reason there is life on Earth.

Journal *Activity*

You and Your World Have you ever thought about being an astronaut? What kind of training do you think you would need to become an astronaut? In what ways do you think life in space would be different from life on Earth? Draw a picture in your journal of what you think it would be like to float in space and describe some of the conditions you would expect to encounter.

Towering clouds are a familiar sight in the Earth's atmosphere.

1–1 A View of Planet Earth: Spheres Within a Sphere

Have you ever seen a carved doll like the one in Figure 1–1? This doll holds some surprises within its painted wooden shell. When it is opened you can see that what appeared to be a single doll is actually a series of dolls, snugly nesting one within the other. These sets of dolls are made in Russia and are part of the folk heritage of the Russian people.

In some ways, the Earth is similar to this set of dolls. What appears to be a simple structure is, upon close examination, found to have many hidden layers of complexity. And along with this complexity comes a kind of awe-inspiring beauty.

Size of the Earth

Exactly how large is planet Earth? Its size can be described by two measurements: its diameter and its circumference. The diameter of the Earth (or the distance from the North Pole to the South Pole through the center) is about 12,740 kilometers. When compared with Jupiter, the largest planet in the solar system with a diameter of 142,700 kilometers, the Earth may not seem to be very large at all. But the Earth is the largest of the inner planets—Mercury, Venus, Earth, and Mars—in the solar system. The diameter of Mars, for example, is only about one-half the diameter of the Earth.

The circumference of the Earth, or the distance around the Earth, is about 40,075 kilometers at the **equator.** The equator is an imaginary line around Earth that divides Earth into two **hemispheres.** These hemispheres are called the Northern Hemisphere and the Southern Hemisphere. In which hemisphere do you live?

Features of the Earth: The Lithosphere, Hydrosphere, and Atmosphere

The word earth has many meanings. It can mean the ground you walk on or the soil in which plants grow. Most importantly, the word Earth can mean

Figure 1–1 *Dolls such as these are part of Russian folk heritage. In what way are these dolls similar to planet Earth?*

Figure 1–2 *In this shot of Earth from space you can see the atmosphere, land areas, and oceans. How much greater is the Earth's circumference than its diameter?*

your planet home. Looking at the Earth from space—actually a relatively new way to view the planet—you can appreciate its extraordinary beauty. You can also observe the three main features that make up your "home."

Photographs from space show that the Earth is a beautiful planet indeed. From space the Earth's land areas can be seen easily. The outlines of continents, in the past seen only as two-dimensional drawings on a map, become real when photographed by satellite cameras. From space, the oceans and other bodies of water that cover much of the Earth can clearly be identified. In fact, about 70 percent of the Earth's surface is covered by water. From space, the Earth's atmosphere can be observed, if only indirectly. The clouds in the photograph in Figure 1–2, floating freely above land and water, are part of the normally invisible atmosphere that surrounds the Earth.

The three main features of the Earth are the land, the water, and the air. The land areas of the Earth are part of a solid layer of the Earth known as the crust. Land areas include the seven continents and all other landmasses. Such land areas are clearly visible as part of the Earth's surface. But there is also land that is not visible—land that exists beneath the oceans and beneath the continents. You will learn more about this solid layer of the Earth in Chapter 4. Scientists call all the land on Earth the **lithosphere,** a word that means "rock-sphere." Why do you think this is an appropriate name?

The water on Earth makes up the **hydrosphere.** (The prefix *hydro-* means water.) The hydrosphere includes the Earth's oceans, rivers and streams, ponds and lakes, seas and bays, and other bodies of water. Some of the hydrosphere is frozen in the polar ice caps at the North and South poles, as well as in icebergs and glaciers.

You might be surprised to learn that about 97 percent of the hydrosphere is composed of salt water. The most common salt in salt water is sodium chloride, which you are more familiar with as table salt. You might think that the remaining 3 percent

FACTS ABOUT THE EARTH

Average distance from sun
About 150,000,000 kilometers

Diameter through equator
12,756.32 kilometers

Circumference around equator
40,075.16 kilometers

Surface area
Land area, about 148,300,000 square kilometers, or about 30 percent of total surface area; water area, about 361,800,000 square kilometers, or about 70 percent of total surface area

Rotation period
23 hours, 56 minutes, 4.09 seconds

Revolution period around sun
365 days, 6 hours, 9 minutes, 9.54 seconds

Temperature
Highest, 58°C at Al Aziziyah, Libya; lowest, -90°C at Vostok in Antarctica; average surface temperature, 14°C

Highest and lowest land features
Highest, Mount Everest, 8848 meters above sea level; lowest, shore of Dead Sea, 396 meters below sea level

Ocean depths
Deepest, Mariana Trench in Pacific Ocean southwest of Guam, 11,033 meters below surface; average ocean depth, 3795 meters

Figure 1–3 *These unusual rock formations in Canyonlands National Park, Utah, are part of the Earth's crust.*

of the hydrosphere is fresh water that can be used by humans for a variety of purposes. You would not be correct, however. Almost 85 percent of the fresh water on Earth exists as ice locked up in the great polar ice caps. That leaves about 15 percent of the 3 percent as liquid fresh water. And keep in mind that this liquid fresh water is not evenly distributed over the Earth. The deserts of the Earth have very little fresh water, whereas the tropical areas have a great

Figure 1–4 *Don't let this creek in California fool you. Most of the Earth's fresh water is locked up in the great polar ice caps. Here you see the southern polar cap in Antarctica. To which sphere does the Earth's fresh and salt water belong?*

deal. Remember also that it is liquid water that makes life on this planet possible. Without water, no life would exist on Earth.

The oxygen that you breathe is found in the last great sphere that makes up planet Earth, the **atmosphere** (AT-muhs-feer). The atmosphere is the envelope of gases that surrounds the Earth. The atmosphere protects the Earth and also provides materials necessary to support all forms of life on the Earth. In the next three sections, you will learn more about Earth's atmosphere. In later chapters, you will learn about the other spheres of planet Earth.

1–1 Section Review

1. What are the three main features of the Earth?
2. What percentage of the hydrosphere is fresh water? What percentage of the hydrosphere is available for drinking?
3. What is the envelope of gases that surrounds the Earth called?

Connection—*Astronomy*

4. *Viking* was the name of the lander that explored the surface of Mars. One of its primary missions was to determine if life existed there. What one test do you think *Viking* performed in order to get an answer to this question?

ACTIVITY

///// READING

Explorers of the Atmosphere—and Beyond

The last half of the twentieth century has witnessed the fulfillment of many dreams. During this time, brave women and men have taken the first tentative steps in exploring space. You might like to read *The Right Stuff*, by Tom Wolfe. This book details early attempts by the United States to explore the frontiers of air and space travel, and contains the "stuff" that dreams are made of.

1–2 Development of the Atmosphere

When astronauts walk in space, they must wear space suits. The space suits provide a protective covering. They enclose the astronauts in an artificial environment, providing them with comfortable temperatures as well as with moisture and oxygen. Space suits also protect the astronauts from harmful ultraviolet rays given off by the sun. In a similar way, the atmosphere of the Earth provides protection for you. And it also provides some of the materials necessary to support life on Earth.

Guide for Reading

Focus on these questions as you read.

▶ *How does the atmosphere on Earth today compare with the atmosphere long ago?*

▶ *What gases are present in the atmosphere?*

Cameras and other instruments aboard space satellites have provided much data about the structure and composition of the present atmosphere. From this information, and from other studies, scientists have developed a picture of what the Earth's atmosphere may have been like billions of years ago. Scientists are certain that the atmosphere of the Earth has changed greatly over time. And they believe that the present atmosphere is still changing! What are some of the conditions that may be responsible for changes in the atmosphere?

The Past Atmosphere

It is theorized that the Earth's atmosphere 4 billion years ago contained two deadly gases: methane and ammonia. Methane, which is made up of the elements carbon and hydrogen, is a poisonous compound. Ammonia, also poisonous, is composed of the elements nitrogen and hydrogen. There was also some water in the atmosphere 4 billion years ago.

As you well know, the air is no longer deadly. In fact, you could not live without it. How did this important change in the atmosphere occur?

To explain this change, it is necessary to picture the atmosphere 3.8 billion years ago. At that time, sunlight triggered chemical reactions among the methane, ammonia, and water in the air. As a result

Figure 1–5 *Scientists use a variety of tools to study the atmosphere, including weather balloons and satellites orbiting in space. Gases trapped in the ice caps thousands of years ago provide scientists with a glimpse of Earth's ancient atmosphere.*

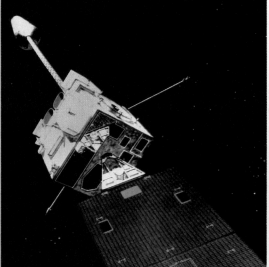

Figure 1–6 *An artist's idea of what the Earth may have looked like billions of years ago. What two deadly gases were common in the ancient atmosphere?*

of many chemical reactions, new materials formed in the atmosphere. Among the new materials were nitrogen, hydrogen, and carbon dioxide. The methane and ammonia broke down, but the water still remained.

Hydrogen is a very lightweight gas, so lightweight in fact, that it escaped the pull of the Earth's gravity and disappeared into space. That left nitrogen in greatest abundance, as well as carbon dioxide and water vapor. In the upper parts of the ancient atmosphere, sunlight began to break down the water vapor into hydrogen and oxygen gases. The lightweight hydrogen gas again escaped into space. But, the atoms of oxygen gas began to combine with one another to form a gas known as **ozone.** Eventually a layer of ozone gas formed about 30 kilometers above the Earth's surface.

The ozone layer is sometimes referred to as an "umbrella" for life on Earth. This is because the ozone layer absorbs most of the harmful ultraviolet radiation from the sun. Without the protection of the ozone layer, few living things could survive on Earth.

Before the ozone layer formed, the only living things on Earth were microscopic organisms that lived far below the surface of the oceans. Here these

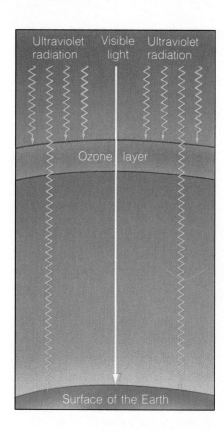

Ultraviolet radiation | Visible light | Ultraviolet radiation

Ozone layer

Surface of the Earth

Figure 1–7 *The ozone layer absorbs most of the sun's harmful ultraviolet radiation before it reaches the Earth's surface. Visible light is not absorbed by the ozone layer.*

organisms were protected from most of the ultraviolet radiation from the sun. After the formation of the ozone layer, certain types of microorganisms called blue-green bacteria started to appear on or near the water's surface. These bacteria used the energy in sunlight to combine carbon dioxide from the air with water to produce food.

A byproduct of this food-making process would change the planet forever. This byproduct was oxygen. Unlike ozone, which formed high in the atmosphere, oxygen remained near the surface of the Earth. It would be this oxygen that animals would later breathe.

In time, green plants began to grow on the land. And they, too, took in carbon dioxide and released oxygen during the food-making process. The oxygen content in the atmosphere increased greatly. Then, around 600 million years ago, the amounts of oxygen and carbon dioxide in the atmosphere began to level off. Since that time, the composition of the atmosphere has remained fairly constant.

Figure 1–8 *Billions of years ago, microscopic organisms such as blue-green bacteria helped to change the Earth's atmosphere by producing oxygen as a byproduct of their food-making process. This increase in the oxygen levels in the atmosphere permitted the evolution of green plants and eventually the animals that feed on green plants.*

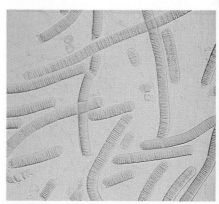

The Present Atmosphere

The atmosphere that surrounds the Earth today contains the gases necessary for the survival of living things. The air you breathe is among the Earth's most important natural resources. What is the air made of?

The atmosphere is a mixture of gases. **The atmospheric gases include nitrogen, oxygen, carbon dioxide, water vapor, argon, and trace gases.** Nitrogen gas makes up about 78 percent of the atmosphere. Another 21 percent of the atmosphere is oxygen. The remaining 1 percent is a combination of carbon dioxide, water vapor, argon, and trace gases. Among the trace gases, which are present in only very small amounts, are neon, helium, krypton, and xenon.

NITROGEN The most abundant gas in the atmosphere is nitrogen. Living things need nitrogen to make proteins. Proteins are complex compounds that contain nitrogen. These compounds are required for the growth and repair of body parts. The muscles of your body are made mostly of protein, as are parts of the skin and internal organs.

Figure 1-9 *This diagram shows the nitrogen cycle. How is nitrogen returned to the soil?*

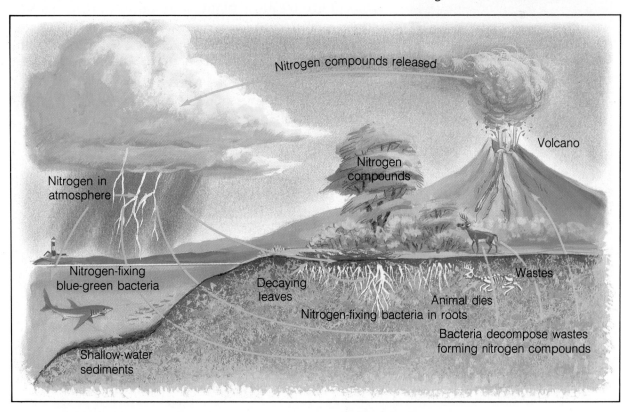

Nitrogen compounds released

Volcano

Nitrogen in atmosphere

Nitrogen compounds

Nitrogen-fixing blue-green bacteria

Decaying leaves

Wastes

Animal dies

Nitrogen-fixing bacteria in roots

Bacteria decompose wastes forming nitrogen compounds

Shallow-water sediments

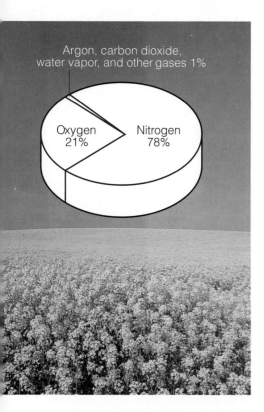

Argon, carbon dioxide, water vapor, and other gases 1%

Oxygen 21%

Nitrogen 78%

Figure 1-10 *The atmosphere is a mixture of many gases. Which two gases make up most of the Earth's atmosphere?*

However, plants and animals are not able to use the nitrogen in the air directly to make proteins. Certain kinds of bacteria that live in the soil are able to combine the nitrogen from the atmosphere with other chemicals to make compounds called nitrates. These bacteria are called nitrogen-fixing bacteria. Plants are able to use the nitrates formed by the nitrogen-fixing bacteria to make plant proteins. In turn, animals get the proteins they need by eating plants.

Nitrogen is returned to the atmosphere when dead animals and plants decay. Decay is the breaking down of dead organisms, usually by bacteria, into simple chemical substances. Thus the organisms that bring about decay return the nitrogen to the atmosphere. The movement of nitrogen from the atmosphere to the soil then to living things and finally back to the atmosphere makes up the nitrogen cycle.

OXYGEN Oxygen is the second most abundant gas in the atmosphere. Oxygen is used directly from the atmosphere by most plants and animals. It is essential for respiration (rehs-puh-RAY-shuhn). During respiration, living things chemically combine oxygen with food. This breaks down the food and releases the energy needed by living things. Why do you think all living things need energy?

Oxygen is also necessary for the combustion, or burning, of fuels such as oil, coal, and wood. Combustion will not take place without oxygen. This is why many fire extinguishers contain special chemicals to fight fires. When sprayed on a fire, the chemicals prevent oxygen from reaching the burning material and supporting any further combustion. Without oxygen, the fire goes out.

CARBON DIOXIDE The amount of carbon dioxide in the atmosphere is very small. However, carbon dioxide is one of the important raw materials used by green plants to make food.

Carbon dioxide is removed from the atmosphere by plants during the food-making process. It is returned to the atmosphere by the respiration of

Figure 1-11 *Bacteria and other decay organisms play an important role, as they remove nitrogen and other substances from dead organisms and return these chemicals to the environment.*

Figure 1–12 on the diagram:
Carbon dioxide used by plants
Carbon dioxide given off by animals
Carbon dioxide given off by decaying leaves
Oxygen given off by plants
Oxygen used by animals
Oxygen from food-making process available to animals
Carbon dioxide from respiration available to plants

plants and animals. The decay of dead plants and animals also returns carbon dioxide to the air.

Scientists believe that the amount of carbon dioxide used by plants equals the amount returned to the atmosphere by respiration, decay, and other natural processes. But the burning of fossil fuels such as oil and coal is adding even more carbon dioxide to the atmosphere. Scientists are concerned that the amount of carbon dioxide in the atmosphere is increasing to a level that may become dangerous. Studies have shown that the increased level of carbon dioxide traps more of the sun's heat energy in the Earth's atmosphere. Thus an increase in the level of carbon dioxide in the air could significantly increase the overall temperature of the Earth.

WATER VAPOR Water vapor in the atmosphere plays an important role in the Earth's weather. Clouds, fog, and dew are weather conditions caused by water vapor in the air. Rain and other forms of precipitation (snow, sleet, and hail) occur when water vapor forms droplets that are heavy enough to fall. Water vapor is also involved in the heating of the atmosphere. Water vapor absorbs heat energy given off by the sun. The amount of water vapor in

Figure 1–12 *Carbon dioxide and oxygen are continuously exchanged among plants and animals. How is oxygen returned to the atmosphere?*

Figure 1–13 *Where would you find more water vapor in the atmosphere—in a rain forest in Hawaii or the sand dunes of the Sahara?*

Activity Bank

A Model of Acid Rain, p.166

ACTIVITY

DISCOVERING

Clean Air Anyone?

1. Spread a thin layer of petroleum jelly on each of three clean microscope slides. With your teacher's permission, place the slides in different locations in and around your school building. Leave the slides in place for several days.

2. Collect the slides and examine each one under a microscope. Count the particles you find. Draw what you observe.

Where was the slide with the fewest particles placed? Where was the slide with the most particles placed?

■ How can you account for the differences?

the atmosphere varies from place to place. In desert regions, the amount of water vapor in the air is usually very small, although most deserts have rainy seasons that last for short periods of time. In tropical regions, the amount of water vapor in the air may be as high as 4 percent. Where else on Earth would you expect to find a great deal of water vapor in the atmosphere?

SOLID PARTICLES Many tiny particles of solid material are mixed with the air's gases. These particles are so small that they can float on even the slightest movements of the air. You may have noticed these particles if you have observed a flashlight beam in a darkened room. These particles in the air are dust, smoke, dirt, and even tiny bits of salt. Where do these particles come from?

Every time a wave breaks, tiny particles of salt from ocean water enter the atmosphere and remain suspended in the air. Much of the dust in the air comes from the eruption of volcanoes. In 1883, the massive eruption of Krakatoa, a volcano in the East Indies, spewed huge amounts of volcanic dust and other materials into the air. As a result of this eruption, skies as far away as London became dark. The average temperature of the Earth fell 1.5°C as volcanic dust from this single eruption filled the air, preventing sunlight from warming the atmosphere. Dirt and smoke particles are also added to the air by

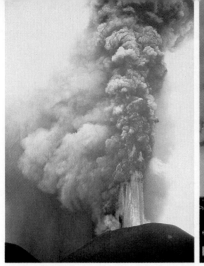

Figure 1–14 *Volcanoes and factories that burn fossil fuels add solid particles to the atmosphere. How are these bikers in Holland helping to keep the Earth's atmosphere a bit cleaner?*

the actions of people as they burn fuels, and as they drive cars and other vehicles. Factories and power plants that burn fossil fuels also add particles to the air. However, new kinds of smoke stacks reduce the amount of particles being added to the air by actually "scrubbing" the smoke before it is released into the air. Do you have any suggestions about what you and your family and friends can do to reduce the amounts of these particles that affect the quality of the air?

Figure 1–15 *Some pollutants found in the atmosphere include asbestos particles (top) and ash from burning coal (bottom).*

1–2 Section Review

1. What two gases were present in the greatest amounts in the atmosphere of Earth 4 billion years ago?
2. What four gases are present in the greatest amounts in the Earth's atmosphere today?
3. Describe the nitrogen cycle and the water cycle. Why is it important that certain substances in the atmosphere are used over and over again?
4. Why are scientists concerned that the level of carbon dioxide in the air is increasing?

Critical Thinking—*Relating Cause and Effect*
5. How have living organisms changed the composition of the atmosphere over time?

Protection From the Sun

All life on Earth depends upon the sun. But the sun also poses certain dangers. You learned that the ozone layer acts like a shield that protects organisms on Earth from some of the dangerous radiation given off by the sun. Newspaper and magazine articles, television and radio programs issue warnings—on an almost daily basis—of the dangers posed to the ozone layer by certain chemicals. This graph shows the effects of limiting the release of ozone-damaging chemicals into the atmosphere.

Interpreting Graphs

1. How has the amount of ozone-damaging chemicals changed from 1975 to 1985?

2. What amount of ozone-damaging chemicals is projected to be in the atmosphere in 1995?

3. How does this amount compare with the amount in the atmosphere today?

4. Two meetings proposed controls on the amount of ozone-damaging chemicals that could be released into the atmosphere. What would happen to the amounts of ozone-damaging chemicals released in the air in 2005 according to the London agreement? According to the Montreal agreement?

■ Which agreement offers some protection for the ozone layer?

5. On Your Own Find out what you can do to limit the amounts of ozone-damaging chemicals that are released into the air.

ATTACK ON THE OZONE SHIELD

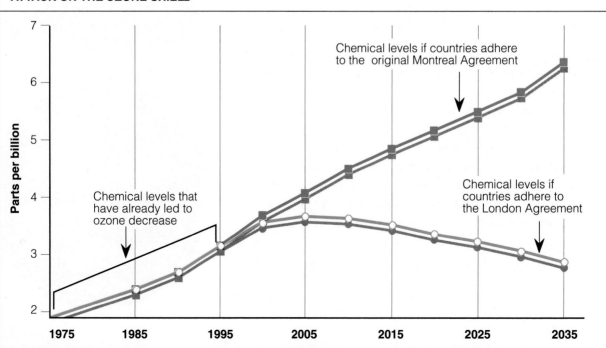

Chemical levels if countries adhere to the original Montreal Agreement

Chemical levels if countries adhere to the London Agreement

Chemical levels that have already led to ozone decrease

Parts per billion

1975   1985   1995   2005   2015   2025   2035

1–3 Layers of the Atmosphere

Guide for Reading

Focus on this question as you read.

▶ How are the layers in the atmosphere related to temperature?

If you were able to soar up from the surface of the Earth to the high edge of outer space, you would notice many changes in the atmosphere. The mixture of gases, the temperature, and the electrical and magnetic forces of the atmosphere change as the distance from the Earth's surface increases. For example, there is less oxygen in the upper atmosphere than in the lower atmosphere. You may have seen pictures of mountain climbers wearing oxygen masks when they were climbing very high mountains. They do this because there is only half as much oxygen available 5.5 kilometers above the Earth's surface as there is at the Earth's surface.

If you ever climb a high mountain yourself, you will notice that as you climb upward the air gets colder. At an altitude (height above sea level) of 3 kilometers, you will probably need a heavy jacket to keep warm! The temperature of the air decreases as the altitude increases because the air becomes less dense. That is, there are fewer and fewer particles of air in a given amount of space. The thin, less dense air cannot hold as much heat.

The atmosphere is divided into layers according to major changes in its temperature. The layers of air that surround the Earth are held close to it by the force of gravity. Gravity is a force of attraction by which objects are pulled toward each other. Because of gravity, the layers of air surrounding the Earth push down on the Earth's surface. This push is called **air pressure.**

The upper layers of air push down on the lower layers. So the air pressure near the surface of the Earth is greater than the air pressure further from the surface. If you have ever flown in an airplane, you may have felt your ears "pop." This popping was caused by a change in air pressure. Where else might you experience a change in air pressure?

It is interesting to note that 99 percent of the total mass of the atmosphere of the Earth is below an altitude of 32 kilometers. The remaining 1 percent of the atmosphere's mass is in the hundreds of kilometers above an altitude of 32 kilometers.

AIR PRESSURE AND ALTITUDE

Altitude (meters)	Air Pressure (g/cm^2)
Sea level	1034
3000	717
6000	450
9000	302
12,000	190
15,000	112

Figure 1–16 *Climbers need warm clothing and oxygen masks on a high mountain because the air is colder and thinner (less dense). How does air pressure change as altitude increases?*

Figure 1-17 *Convection currents in the atmosphere, caused by heat from the sun, contribute to the Earth's weather. In what layer of the atmosphere does most weather occur?*

ACTIVITY

DISCOVERING

The Temperature Plot

1. At three times during both the day and evening, use an outdoor thermometer to measure air temperature 1 centimeter above the ground and 1.25 meters above the ground. Record the time of day and the temperature for both locations.

2. On graph paper, plot time (X axis) versus temperature (Y axis) for each thermometer location. Label both graphs.

In which area did the temperature change most rapidly? In which area did the temperature change a greater amount over the entire time period?

■ Why do you think the temperatures changed as they did?

Now let's pretend that you are able to soar upward from the Earth's surface through the levels of the atmosphere. What will each layer look and feel like? Read on to find out.

The Troposphere

The layer of the atmosphere closest to Earth is the **troposphere** (TRO-po-sfeer). It is the layer in which you live. Almost all of the Earth's weather occurs in the troposphere.

The height of the troposphere varies from the equator to the poles. Around the equator, the height of the troposphere is about 17 kilometers. In areas north and south of the equator, the height is about 12 kilometers. At the poles, the troposphere extends upward between 6 and 8 kilometers.

As the heat energy from sunlight travels through the atmosphere, only a small amount of the heat energy is trapped by the atmosphere. Most of the heat energy is absorbed by the ground. The ground then warms the air above it. Warm air is less dense than cool air. The warm, less dense air rises and is replaced by cooler, denser air. Currents of air that carry heat up into the atmosphere are produced.

These air movements are called **convection** (kuhn-VEHK-shuhn) **currents.** You might be familiar with convection currents if you have observed a convection oven in use. This kind of oven contains a fan that continuously moves the hot oven air over the food. Food cooks more quickly and evenly in a convection oven than in a conventional oven.

Remember that temperature decreases with increasing altitude because the air becomes less dense. The temperature of the troposphere drops about 6.5°C for every kilometer above the Earth's surface. However, at an altitude of about 12 kilometers, the temperature seems to stop dropping. The zone of the troposphere where the temperature remains fairly constant is called the tropopause (TRO-po-pawz). The tropopause divides the troposphere from the next layer of the atmosphere.

The Stratosphere

The **stratosphere** (STRAT-uh-sfeer) extends from the tropopause to an altitude of about 50 kilometers. In the lower stratosphere, the temperature of the air remains constant and extremely cold— around −60°C. This temperature equals the coldest temperature ever recorded in a location other than Antarctica. It was recorded in Snag, in the Yukon Territory, Canada. The world's coldest recorded temperature, −90°C, occurred in Vostok, Antarctica.

The air in the lower stratosphere is not still. Here very strong eastward winds blow horizontally around the Earth. These winds, called the **jet stream,** reach speeds of more than 320 kilometers per hour. What effect do you think jet streams have on weather patterns in the United States?

A special form of oxygen called ozone is present in the stratosphere. Ozone has a clean sharp smell. You have probably smelled ozone after a thunderstorm or when you are near an electric motor that is running. In both cases ozone forms when electricity passes through the atmosphere. In the case of a thunderstorm, the electricity is in the form of lightning.

Most of the ozone in the atmosphere is found in the ozone layer located between 16 kilometers and

Figure 1–18 *A jet stream forms where cold air from the poles meets warmer air from the equator. This high-altitude jet stream is moving over the Nile Valley and the Red Sea.*

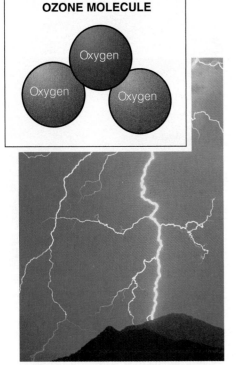

OZONE MOLECULE

Oxygen

Oxygen

Oxygen

Figure 1–19 *The ozone layer forms a protective umbrella in the stratosphere. Ozone, a molecule made up of three oxygen atoms, is formed when lightning passes through the atmosphere.*

ACTIVITY

CALCULATING

How Thick Are the Atmosphere's Layers?

Figure 1–20 shows the layers of the Earth's atmosphere and the altitudes at which they begin and end. Use the information in the diagram to calculate the average thickness of each layer.

60 kilometers above the surface of the Earth. Below and above these altitudes, there is little or no ozone. Although the total amount of ozone in the stratosphere is actually very small, ozone is extremely important to life on Earth. Ozone acts as a shield for the Earth's surface. As you learned in the previous section, ozone absorbs most of the ultraviolet radiation from the sun. Ultraviolet radiation is harmful to living things. Overexposure of the skin to ultraviolet radiation (often in the form of a bad sunburn) has been linked to skin cancer.

You may already know that you can get a bad sunburn on a cloudy day, even when it seems as if little sunlight is reaching the Earth. Ultraviolet rays are able to pass through cloud layers. In some ways, the ozone layer acts like a sunblock. Without it, more of the sun's harmful ultraviolet radiation would reach the Earth's surface, and you would always be in great danger of being badly burned by the sun's rays.

Ozone is also responsible for the increase in temperature that occurs in the upper stratosphere. Heat is given off as ozone reacts with ultraviolet radiation. This heat warms the upper stratosphere to temperatures around 18°C. The zone in which the temperature is at its highest is called the stratopause (STRAT-uh-pawz). The stratopause separates the stratosphere from the next layer of the atmosphere.

The Mesosphere

Above the stratopause, the temperature begins to decrease. This drop in temperature marks the beginning of the **mesosphere** (MEHS-oh-sfeer). The mesosphere extends from about 50 kilometers to about 80 kilometers above the Earth's surface. The temperature in the mesosphere drops to about −100°C. The upper region of the mesosphere is the coldest region of the atmosphere. If water vapor is present, thin clouds of ice form. You can see these feathery clouds if sunlight strikes them after sunset.

The mesosphere helps protect the Earth from large rocklike objects in space known as meteoroids (MEET-ee-uh-roidz). When meteoroids enter the atmosphere, they burn up in the mesosphere. The heat caused by the friction, or rubbing, between the meteoroid and the atmosphere causes this burning.

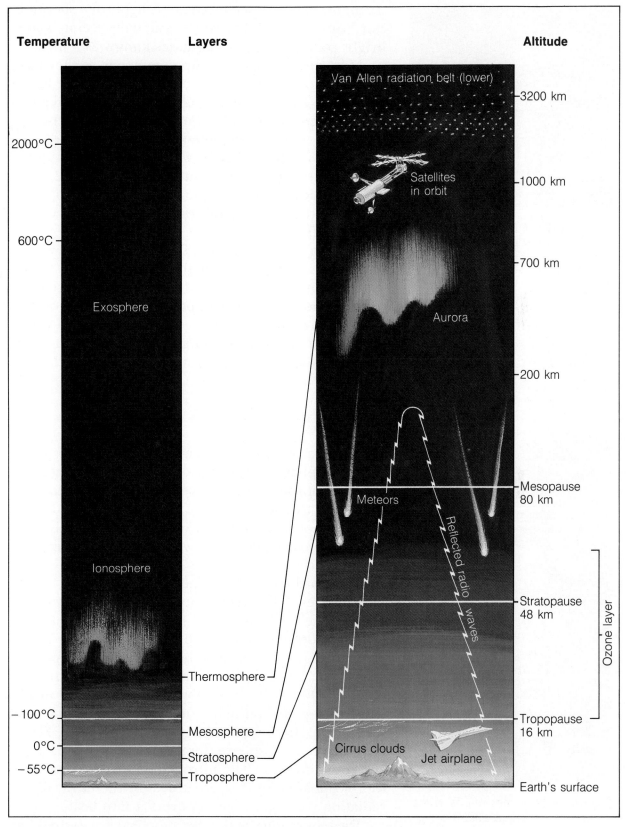

Figure 1–20 *The four main layers of the atmosphere and their characteristics are shown here. In which layer do you live? In which layer is the temperature the highest?*

Figure 1–21 *A meteorite crater in Arizona formed when a meteorite struck the Earth around 20,000 years ago.*

At night, you may see a streak of light, or "shooting star," in the sky. What you are actually seeing is a bright trail of hot, glowing gases known as a meteor.

Most meteoroids burn up completely as they pass through the Earth's atmosphere. But some are large enough to survive the passage and actually strike the Earth. These pieces are called meteorites (MEET-ee-er-rights). A few large meteorites have produced huge craters on the Earth. The most famous is the Barringer meteorite crater in Arizona. It is 1.2 kilometers wide. Scientists estimate that the meteorite that caused this crater fell to the Earth within the last 20,000 years.

When artificial satellites fall from orbit, they also burn up as they pass through the atmosphere. However, pieces of the United States's *Skylab* and the Soviet Union's *Cosmos* satellite have fallen out of orbit and reached the Earth's surface. Why do you think some meteoroids and satellites do not burn up completely as they pass through the layers of the atmosphere?

The Thermosphere

The **thermosphere** (THER-moh-sfeer) begins above the mesosphere at a height of about 80 kilometers. The thermosphere has no well-defined upper limit. The air in the thermosphere is very thin. The density of the atmosphere and the air pressure are only about one ten-millionth of what they are at the Earth's surface.

The word *thermosphere* means "heat sphere," or "warm layer." The temperature is very high in this layer of the atmosphere. In fact, the temperature of the thermosphere may reach 2000°C or more! To give you some idea of how hot this is, the temperature at the bottom of a furnace used to make steel reaches 1900°C. At this temperature, the steel mixture is a liquid! You may wonder why the temperature of the thermosphere is so high. (After all, for most of the atmosphere, temperature decreases as altitude increases.) The nitrogen and oxygen in the thermosphere absorb a great deal of the ultraviolet radiation from space and convert it into heat.

The temperature in the thermosphere is measured with special instruments, not with a thermometer.

Figure 1–22 *Temperatures in the thermosphere reach 2000°C, which is higher than the temperatures in a steel furnace.*

If a thermometer were placed in the thermosphere, it would register far below 0°C! This may seem strange since the thermosphere is so hot. How can this be explained? Temperature is a measurement of how fast particles in the air move. The faster the air particles move, the higher the temperature. And the particles present in the thermosphere are moving very fast. Therefore the particles themselves are very hot.

But these particles are very few and very far apart. There are not enough of them present to bombard a thermometer and warm it. So the thermometer would record a temperature far below 0°C.

THE IONOSPHERE The lower thermosphere is called the **ionosphere** (igh-AHN-uh-sfeer). The ionosphere extends from 80 kilometers to 550 kilometers above the Earth's surface. The size of the ionosphere varies with the amount of ultraviolet and X-ray radiation, two types of invisible energy given off by the sun.

Nitrogen oxides, oxygen, and other gas particles in the ionosphere absorb the ultraviolet radiation and X-rays given off by the sun. The particles of gas become electrically charged. Electrically charged particles are called **ions.** Hence the name ionosphere.

The ions in the ionosphere are important to radio communication. AM radio waves are bounced

Figure 1–23 Radio waves are bounced off the ionosphere to transmit radio messages overseas or across continents. There are three types of waves, and each travels to a different height in the ionosphere. Why do storms on the sun interfere with the transmission of radio waves in the ionosphere?

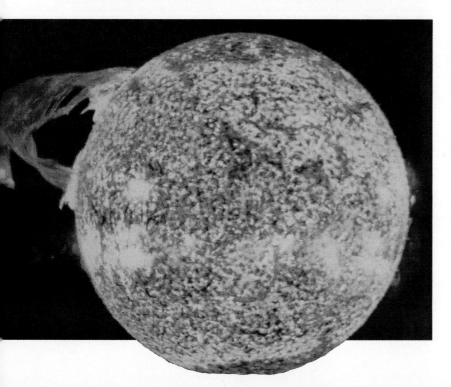

Figure 1–24 *Weather satellites orbiting the Earth transmit information used by scientists to track weather patterns. What type of weather do you think the southeastern United States is having?*

off the ions in the ionosphere and back to the Earth's surface. As a result, AM radio messages can be sent over great distances.

Sometimes large disturbances on the sun's surface, known as solar flares, cause the number of ions in the ionosphere to increase. This increase in ions can interfere with the transmission of some radio waves.

THE EXOSPHERE The upper thermosphere is called the **exosphere** (EHKS-oh-sfeer). The exosphere extends from about 550 kilometers above the Earth's surface for thousands of kilometers. The air is so thin in the exosphere that one particle can travel great distances without hitting another particle.

It is in the exosphere that artificial satellites orbit the Earth. Satellites play an important role in television transmission and in telephone communication. Does it surprise you to learn how great a distance a long distance call actually travels if the signal bounces off a satellite in the exosphere before it returns to the Earth? Satellites are also used to keep a 24-hour watch on the world's weather. And because the very thin air in the exosphere makes seeing objects in space easier, telescopes are often carried aboard satellites.

1–3 Section Review

1. How are the layers of the atmosphere divided? What are the four main layers?
2. Identify one significant characteristic of each layer of the atmosphere. How is that characteristic important to you on Earth?
3. Why is ozone important to life on Earth?
4. Why is the temperature in the thermosphere not measured with a thermometer?

Connection—*Ecology*

5. Scientists are concerned that "holes" are being created in the ozone layer. In such a hole, the amount of ozone is reduced. Predict what would happen to life on Earth if the amount of ozone in the ozone layer were depleted.

CONNECTIONS

Sneezing and Wheezing— It's Allergy Time

It's spring again. The days get longer. The sun seems warmer and friendlier. Plants once again begin to grow. After the short, cold days of winter, most people look forward to spring as a promise of the season to come. But for many others, spring brings the misery of allergies. An allergy is a reaction caused by an increased sensitivity to a certain substance. With every breath they take, allergy sufferers are reminded of the many natural sources of air pollution.

Pollen grains are one kind of particle normally found in the air. Pollen grains are male plant reproductive cells. During certain times of the year, different kinds of pollen are released into the air. For example, maple and oak trees flower in the early spring, releasing millions upon millions of pollen grains into the air. These pollen grains are lightweight and float on air currents. If a person with an allergy to maple and oak tree pollen breathes in these pollen grains, certain cells in the respiratory system overreact, producing a chemical called histamine. This chemical causes the nose to run, the throat to tickle, and the eyes to water and itch.

You have probably heard of the condition called hay fever. Hay fever is neither a fever nor is it caused by hay. Hay fever is another example of an allergy. In this case, the culprit is ragweed pollen. Ragweed pollen also causes histamine to be produced.

There is no complete cure for allergies. If the particular pollen cannot be avoided, sufferers can take allergy-relief medicines prescribed by their physicians. As you can see, for some people, there are dangers hidden in the beauty of the natural world.

Ragweed pollen (left), ragweed plant (right)

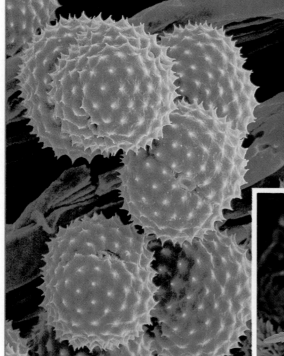

1–4 The Magnetosphere

The area around the Earth that extends beyond the atmosphere is called the **magnetosphere** (mag-NEET-oh-sfeer). The Earth's magnetic force operates in the magnetosphere. The magnetosphere begins at an altitude of about 1000 kilometers. On the side of the Earth that faces the sun, the magnetosphere extends out into space about 4000 kilometers. It extends even farther into space on the other side of the Earth. See Figure 1–25. The difference in size of the magnetosphere is caused by the solar wind, which is a stream of fast-moving ions given off by the outermost layer of the sun's atmosphere. (Ions, recall, are electrically charged particles common to the ionosphere.) The solar wind pushes the magnetosphere farther into space on the side of the Earth away from the sun.

The magnetosphere is made up of positively charged protons and negatively charged electrons. Protons and electrons are two of the most important particles that make up atoms. An atom is considered the basic building block of matter, or the smallest unit from which all substances are made. Protons and electrons are given off by the sun and captured by the Earth's magnetic field. The charged particles

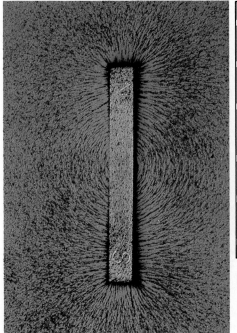

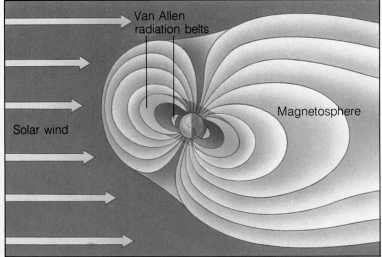

Figure 1–25 *The Earth acts like a giant bar magnet whose lines of force produce the same pattern as a small bar magnet. Why does the magnetosphere formed by the Earth extend farther on one side than on the other?*

Figure 1–26 *Electrically charged particles from the sun collide with particles in the upper atmosphere and produce the multicolored lights called an aurora. Here you see the aurora borealis, or northern lights.*

are concentrated into belts, or layers, of high radiation. These belts are called the **Van Allen radiation belts.** They were discovered by satellites in 1958 and named after James Van Allen, the scientist whose work led to their discovery.

The Van Allen radiation belts pose a problem for space travelers. Space flights have to be programmed to avoid the radiation or suitable protection must be provided for astronauts who travel through the belts. However, the Van Allen belts are important to life on the Earth. They provide protection by trapping other deadly radiation.

When there is a solar flare, the magnetosphere is bombarded by large quantities of electrically charged particles from the sun. These charged particles get trapped in the magnetosphere. Here they collide with other particles in the upper atmosphere. The collisions cause the atmospheric particles to give off light. The multicolored lights are called the aurora borealis, or northern lights, and the aurora australis, or southern lights.

After a heavy bombardment of solar particles, sometimes called a magnetic storm, the magnetic field of the Earth may change temporarily. A compass needle may not point north. Radio signals may be interrupted. Telephone and telegraph communications may also be affected.

1–4 Section Review

1. What is the magnetosphere made of?
2. Why are the Van Allen radiation belts important to life on Earth?
3. How can scientists predict when an aurora will be visible?

Critical Thinking—*Relating Concepts*
4. How did technology contribute to the discovery of the Van Allen radiation belts?

Laboratory Investigation

Radiant Energy and Surface Temperature

Problem

Does the type of surface affect the amount of heat absorbed both in and out of direct sunlight?

Materials (per group)

10 thermometers
stopwatch or clock with sweep second hand
2 shallow containers of water

Procedure 🧪

1. Place a thermometer on the grass in the sun. Place a second thermometer on the grass in the shade.

2. Place the remaining thermometers—one in the sun and one in the shade—on bare soil, on concrete, on a blacktop surface, and in water.

3. After 2 minutes, record the temperature of each surface.

4. Continue recording the temperature of each surface every 2 minutes for a period of 10 minutes.

5. Record your results in a data table similar to the one shown here.

Observations

1. Which surface was the warmest? Which surface was the coolest?

2. By how many degrees did the temperature of each surface in direct sunlight change during the 10-minute time period?

3. By how many degrees did the temperature of each surface in the shade change during the 10-minute period?

Analysis and Conclusions

1. Why do you think the warmest surface was the warmest?

2. How do you explain the temperature change that occurred in water?

3. What conclusions can you reach about the amount of heat energy different surfaces absorb from the sun?

4. **On Your Own**   How can you apply your observations to the kinds of clothing that should be worn in a warm climate? In a cold climate? In what other ways do the results of this investigation affect people's lives?

Surface	Temperature in the Sun					Temperature in the Shade				
	2 min	4 min	6 min	8 min	10 min	2 min	4 min	6 min	8 min	10 min
Grass										
Soil										
Concrete										
Blacktop										
Water										

Summarizing Key Concepts

1–1 A View of Planet Earth: Spheres Within a Sphere

▲ The solid parts of planet Earth make up the lithosphere.

▲ Parts of the Earth that are made up of water compose the hydrosphere.

▲ The envelope of gases that surrounds the Earth is the atmosphere.

1–2 Development of the Atmosphere

▲ About 3.8 billion years ago, chemical reactions triggered by sunlight produced new substances in the atmosphere.

▲ The ozone layer is sometimes referred to as an ''umbrella'' for life on Earth. The ozone layer absorbs much of the harmful radiation from the sun.

▲ The present atmosphere consists mainly of nitrogen, oxygen, carbon dioxide, water vapor, argon, and several other gases present in trace amounts.

1–3 Layers of the Atmosphere

▲ The four main layers of the atmosphere are the troposphere, stratosphere, mesosphere, and the thermosphere.

▲ Almost all of the Earth's weather occurs in the troposphere.

▲ Temperature decreases with increasing altitude in the troposphere. The zone of the troposphere where the temperature remains fairly constant is called the tropopause.

▲ Most of the ozone in the atmosphere is located in a layer of the stratosphere.

▲ The upper mesosphere is the coldest region of the atmosphere.

▲ The thermosphere is made up of the ionosphere and the exosphere.

1–4 The Magnetosphere

▲ The magnetosphere extends from an altitude of about 1000 kilometers far into space.

▲ The Van Allen radiation belts are layers of high radiation that form as a result of the concentration of charged particles.

Reviewing Key Terms

Define each term in a complete sentence.

1–1 A View of Planet Earth: Spheres Within a Sphere
equator
hemisphere
lithosphere
hydrosphere
atmosphere

1–2 Development of the Atmosphere
ozone

1–3 Layers of the Atmosphere
air pressure
troposphere
convection current
stratosphere
jet stream
mesosphere
thermosphere
ionosphere
ion
exosphere

1–4 The Magnetosphere
magnetosphere
Van Allen radiation belt

Chapter Review

Content Review

Multiple Choice

Choose the letter of the answer that best completes each statement.

1. The envelope of gases that surrounds the Earth is called the
   a. lithosphere.
   b. atmosphere.
   c. hydrosphere.
   d. equator.
2. Oceans, lakes, and the polar ice caps are part of the Earth's
   a. crust.
   b. argons.
   c. fresh water.
   d. hydrosphere.
3. Four billion years ago the Earth's atmosphere contained the deadly gases
   a. nitrogen and oxygen.
   b. methane and ammonia.
   c. methane and oxygen.
   d. nitrogen and ozone.
4. The most abundant gas in the atmosphere is
   a. oxygen.
   b. carbon dioxide
   c. argon.
   d. nitrogen.
5. The layer of the atmosphere where the temperature may reach 2000°C is called the
   a. stratosphere.
   b. mesosphere.
   c. thermosphere.
   d. troposphere.
6. Ultraviolet radiation from the sun is absorbed by ozone in the
   a. troposphere.
   b. stratosphere.
   c. thermosphere.
   d. ionosphere.
7. Artificial satellites orbit the Earth in the part of the thermosphere called the
   a. ionosphere.
   b. mesosphere.
   c. exosphere.
   d. troposphere.
8. The lowest layer of the atmosphere is called the
   a. stratosphere.
   b. mesosphere.
   c. thermosphere.
   d. troposphere.

True or False

If the statement is true, write "true." If it is false, change the underlined word or words to make the statement true.

1. Almost 85 percent of the fresh water on Earth is trapped in ice.
2. The envelope of gases that surrounds the Earth is called the hydrosphere.
3. Few living things could survive on Earth without the presence of methane, the gas that absorbs ultraviolet radiation.
4. The magnetosphere is the area that extends beyond the atmosphere.
5. Electrically charged particles are called molecules.
6. As altitude increases, the temperature of the air increases.
7. Because of the increased burning of fossil fuels, the level of carbon dioxide in the air is increasing.

Concept Mapping

Complete the following concept map for Section 1–1. Refer to pages 16–17 to construct a concept map for the entire chapter.

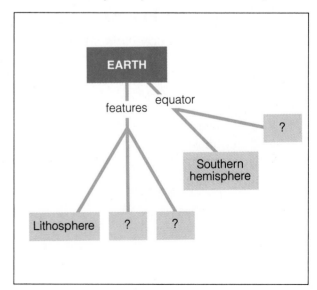

Concept Mastery

Discuss each of the following in a brief paragraph.

1. How did living organisms change the atmosphere of ancient Earth?
2. Tell how each of the following items would be useful for an astronaut on a trip to Mars: a supply of oxygen, a space suit, radiation protection.
3. What are the four most common gases in the troposphere? In what percentages do these gases occur?
4. Explain why air pressure decreases as altitude increases.
5. What is ultraviolet radiation? What effect does this type of radiation have on living things?
6. How have satellites contributed to our knowledge of the atmosphere?

Critical Thinking and Problem Solving

Use the skills you have developed in this chapter to answer each of the following.

1. **Applying concepts** Could animals have lived on ancient Earth before green plants? Explain your answer.
2. **Applying concepts** Traveling from New York to San Francisco, California takes about 5 hours and 30 minutes. The return trip from San Francisco to New York, however, takes about 5 hours. Use your knowledge of the jet stream to explain the difference in travel time.
3. **Relating cause and effect** Scientists are concerned that certain chemicals, when released into the atmosphere, cause the level of ozone to decrease. Predict what might happen to living things on Earth if the ozone layer continues to decrease.
4. **Sequencing events** Make a series of drawings or small dioramas to show how the atmosphere of Earth has changed over time.
5. **Making diagrams** The diagrams on pages 19 and 21 show the nitrogen and the oxygen-carbon dioxide cycles. Use these diagrams as a guide to draw pictures of each cycle as it occurs in your surroundings. Include plants and animals found in your area.
6. **Using the writing process** People have walked on the moon during your parents' or your teachers' lifetime. Conduct an interview with your parents or a teacher. Ask them if they saw the first step onto the moon. Have them describe their feelings at the time of the first moon walk. Organize the information from the interview into a short essay.

Earth's Oceans

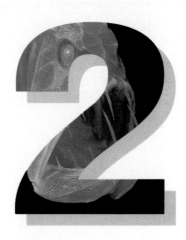

Guide for Reading

After you read the following sections, you will be able to

Many bizarre living things make their home deep beneath the ocean waves. Indeed, some fish look as if they recently swam out of the pages of the strangest science fiction novel. The anoplogaster on the opposite page is but one example. With its needlelike teeth bared, the 15-centimeter fish stalks its prey. Food, however, is scarce in the 6000-meter-deep water this fish calls home.

At this profound depth, the water temperature is near freezing, the pressure tremendous. But in this blue-black ocean water where no sunlight penetrates, the anoplogaster is a fearsome predator.

The oceans are rich in many forms of life. Tiny single-celled plants share the salt waters of the Earth with mammoth whales. A wide variety of organisms obtain the gases and foods they need from ocean water. The ocean plays an important role in your survival, as well. It is a direct source of food and an indirect source of fresh water for all living things.

In this chapter, you will learn more about the oceans—their properties, motions, and the land beneath them. And you will become more familiar with the variety of living things that make the oceans their home.

Journal *Activity*

You and Your World In 1492, it took Christopher Columbus weeks to reach the New World by sailing across the Atlantic in ships powered by winds. Would you have liked to be a member of Columbus's crew? What do you think that long voyage was like? In your journal, keep a diary for a week in which you are a member of Columbus's crew.

Tiny but terrifying, an anoplogaster patrols the ocean depths in search of food.

2–1 The World's Oceans

Suppose a contest was held in which you were asked to rename the Earth? What would you call it? If you looked at the Earth's surface features from space, you might call it Oceanus. This would probably be a good name to choose because about 71 percent of the Earth's surface is covered by ocean water. In fact, the oceans contain most of the Earth's water—about 97 percent. And although each ocean and sea has a separate name, all of the oceans and seas are actually one continuous body of water.

The Atlantic, Indian, and Pacific oceans are the three major oceans. Smaller bodies of ocean water, such as the Mediterranean Sea, the Black Sea, and the Arctic Ocean, are considered part of the Atlantic Ocean. A sea is a part of an ocean that is nearly surrounded by land. Can you name any other seas?

The Pacific Ocean is the largest ocean on Earth. Its area and volume are greater than those of the Atlantic and Indian oceans combined. The Pacific Ocean is also the deepest ocean. Its average depth is 3940 meters. The Atlantic Ocean is the second largest ocean. The average depth of the Atlantic Ocean is 3350 meters. Although the Indian Ocean is much smaller than the Atlantic, its average depth is greater.

The ocean, which you may already know is made of salt water, plays an important role in the water cycle. During this cycle, the sun's rays heat the surface of the ocean. The heat causes the water to evaporate, or change from the liquid phase to the gas phase. The evaporating water—pure, fresh water—enters the atmosphere as water vapor. The salts remain in the ocean.

Winds carry much of the water vapor over land areas. Some of the water vapor in the atmosphere condenses to form clouds. Under the right conditions, the water in clouds falls as precipitation (rain, snow, sleet, and hail). Some of this water runs into

Figure 2–1 *Notice the sea stacks that have been carved by ocean waves off Big Sur in California. What percent of the Earth's surface is covered by water?*

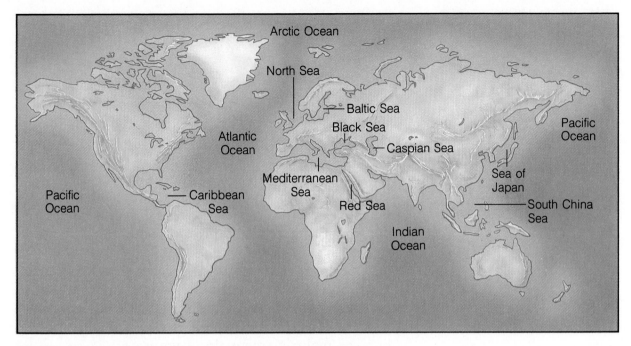

Figure 2–2 *The major oceans and seas of the world are actually part of one continuous body of water. What are the three major oceans?*

rivers and streams that flow directly back into the ocean. Some of it seeps deep into the soil and rocks of the Earth to become part of the groundwater beneath the Earth's surface. As you can see, the ocean is a source of fresh water for all living things.

2–1 Section Review

1. What are the three main oceans of the world?
2. What is a sea?
3. What part does the ocean play as a source of fresh water for all living things?

Critical Thinking—*Relating Cause and Effect*

4. The state of Washington lies on the Pacific Ocean. Certain parts of this state receive large amounts of rain throughout the year. Predict which parts receive the most rain. Explain why.

ACTIVITY

A Salty Tale

In the past, many people who did not eat seafood experienced an enlargement of the thyroid gland. The thyroid is a gland located in the neck that regulates how food is used by the body. This enlargement, called a goiter, results from a lack of a chemical in the body, a chemical commonly found in seafoods. You might like to look up this disease in a library to find out the name of this chemical. Find out what other food this chemical is commonly added to. Report on your findings to the class.

Guide for Reading

Focus on these questions as you read.

- *What is ocean water composed of?*
- *What are some characteristics of ocean water?*

Figure 2–3 *Ocean water is composed of hydrogen, oxygen, and about 85 other elements. Of those other elements, which two are the most abundant?*

MAJOR ELEMENTS IN OCEAN WATER	
Element	**Percent of Total (%)**
Oxygen Hydrogen	96.5
Chlorine	1.9
Sodium	1.1
Magnesium Sulfur Calcium Potassium Bromine Carbon Strontium Silicon Fluorine Aluminum Phosphorus Iodine	0.5
	100

2–2 Properties of Ocean Water

Ocean water is a mixture of gases and solids dissolved in pure water. Scientists who study the ocean, or **oceanographers** (oh-shuh-NAHG-ruh-fuhrz), believe that ocean water contains all of the natural elements found on Earth. Ninety elements are known to exist in nature. So far, about 85 of these have been found in ocean water. Oceanographers are hopeful that with improved technology, they will find the remaining elements.

Ocean water is about 96 percent pure water, or H_2O. So the most abundant elements in ocean water are hydrogen (H) and oxygen (O). The other 4 percent consists of dissolved elements. Figure 2–3 lists the major elements in ocean water.

Salts in Ocean Water

Sodium chloride is the most abundant salt in ocean water. If you have ever accidentally swallowed a mouthful of ocean water, you have probably recognized the taste of sodium chloride. Sodium chloride is, in fact, common table salt. It is made of the elements sodium and chlorine.

Sodium chloride is only one of many salts dissolved in ocean water. Figure 2–4 shows the other salts. Oceanographers use the term **salinity** (suh-LIHN-uh-tee) to describe the amount of dissolved salts in ocean water. Salinity is the number of grams of dissolved salts in 1 kilogram of ocean water. When 1 kilogram of ocean water evaporates, 35 grams of salts remain. Of these 35 grams, 27.2 grams are sodium chloride. How many grams are magnesium chloride?

The salinity of ocean water is expressed in parts per thousand. It ranges between 33 and 37 parts per thousand. The average salinity of ocean water is 35 parts per thousand.

Salts and other materials dissolved in ocean water come from several different sources. One important source is volcanic activity in the ocean. When volcanoes erupt, rock materials and gases spew forth. These substances dissolve in ocean water. Chlorine

Figure 2–4 *The pie chart shows the amounts, in parts per thousand, of the seven most abundant salts in ocean water. What three salts are the most common?*

Water 96.5%

Salts 3.5%

Sodium chloride	27.2 0/00
Magnesium chloride	3.8 0/00
Magnesium sulfate	1.7 0/00
Calcium sulfate	1.3 0/00
Potassium sulfate	0.9 0/00
Calcium carbonate	0.1 0/00
Magnesium bromide	0.1 0/00

gas is one substance that is added to ocean water as a result of volcanic activity.

Another source of dissolved materials is the erosion of the land by rivers, streams, and glaciers. As rivers, streams, and glaciers move over rocks and soil, they dissolve salts in them. Sodium, magnesium, and potassium reach the ocean in this way.

The action of waves breaking along the shore is also a source of salts and other dissolved materials. As waves pound the shoreline, they dissolve the salts contained in the rocks along the coast.

In most areas of the ocean, the salinity is about the same. But in some areas, greater or lesser amounts of dissolved salts cause differences in the salinity. Several reasons explain these differences. The salinity is much lower in areas where freshwater rivers run into the ocean. This is especially true where major rivers such as the Mississippi, Amazon, and Congo flow into the ocean. Can you suggest a reason for the lower salinity? At these points, huge amounts of fresh water pour into the ocean, diluting the normal amount of salts in the ocean water.

In warm ocean areas where there is little rainfall and much evaporation, the amount of dissolved salts in the water is greater than average. Thus, the salinity is higher. The salinity is higher in the polar regions also. Here temperatures are cold enough for

ACTIVITY
DOING

Temperature and Salinity

1. Pour 100 mL of hot tap water into a glass.

2. Add salt, one teaspoonful at a time, to the water. Stir the water after each addition. Stop adding salt when no more can be dissolved. Record the number of teaspoons of salt added. Empty the contents of the glass. Wash the glass.

3. Now pour 100 mL of cold water into the same glass. Repeat steps 1 and 2.

In which glass did more salt dissolve?

What relationship have you illustrated by doing this investigation?

Figure 2-5 *One source of minerals in ocean water is the erosion of cliffs by ocean waves.*

Figure 2-6 *The salinity of the ocean is fairly constant. However, in areas where rivers dump sediment-laden fresh water into the ocean, the salinity is reduced. Ocean animals such as flame scallops also reduce salinity.*

ocean water to freeze. When ocean water freezes, pure water is removed and the salts are left behind.

Scientists believe that the salinity of ocean water is also affected by animal life. Animals such as clams and oysters use calcium salts to build their shells. They remove these salts from ocean water, thus lowering the salinity of the water.

Gases in Ocean Water

The most abundant gases dissolved in ocean water are nitrogen, carbon dioxide, and oxygen. Two of these gases, carbon dioxide and oxygen, are vital to ocean life. Most plants take carbon dioxide from the water and use it to make food. In the presence of sunlight, the plants combine carbon dioxide with water to make sugars. During this process, oxygen is released into the water. Plants and animals use oxygen to break down food and provide energy for all life functions.

The amount of nitrogen, carbon dioxide, oxygen, and other gases in ocean water varies with depth. Nitrogen, carbon dioxide, and oxygen are more abundant at the ocean's surface. Here sunlight easily penetrates and plant growth abounds. The abundant plant growth ensures a large supply of oxygen—certainly a great deal more than is found in the depths of the oceans. Can you explain why?

The amount of dissolved gases is also affected by the temperature of ocean water. Warm water holds less dissolved gas than cold water. When ocean water cools, as in the polar regions, it sinks. (Cold water is

denser, or heavier, than warm water.) It carries oxygen-rich water to the ocean depths. As a result, fish and other animals can live in deep parts of the ocean.

Temperature of Ocean Water

The sun is the major source of heat for the ocean. Because solar energy enters the ocean at the surface, the temperature of the water is highest there. Motions of the ocean, such as waves and currents, mix the surface water and transfer the heat downward. The zone where the water is mixed by waves and currents is called the **surface zone.** The surface zone extends to a depth of at least 100 meters. Sometimes it extends as deep as 400 meters.

The temperature of the water remains fairly constant within a surface zone. It does not change much with depth. But the temperature in a surface zone does change with location and with season. Water near the equator is warmer than water in regions farther north and south. Summer water temperatures are warmer than winter water temperatures. For example, the summer water temperature near the surface of the Caribbean Sea may be 26°C. Farther north, off the coast of England, the temperature near the surface may be 15°C. What do you think happens to the water temperature at these two places during the winter?

Below the surface zone the temperature of the water drops very rapidly. This zone of rapid temperature change is called the **thermocline** (THER-moh-klighn). The thermocline does not occur at a specific depth. The season and the flow of ocean currents alter the depth of the thermocline.

The thermocline exists because warm surface water does not easily mix with cold deep water. The difference in the densities of the warm water and the cold water keeps them from mixing. The less dense warm water floats on top of the denser cold water.

The thermocline forms a transition zone between the surface zone and the **deep zone.** The deep zone is an area of extremely cold water that extends from the bottom of the thermocline to depths of 4000 meters or more. Within the deep zone, the temperature decreases only slightly. At depths greater than

ACTIVITY

DISCOVERING

A Drink of Water

■ Use your knowledge of the properties of salt water to devise a procedure for obtaining fresh water from ocean water by freezing. Describe the steps to your teacher. With permission, try your procedure using the following: Dissolve 3 grams of table salt in 100 mL of water. Report your results to your class.

Figure 2–7 *There are three temperature zones in the ocean.*

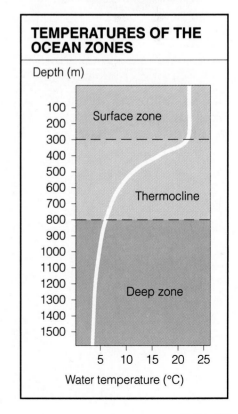

TEMPERATURES OF THE OCEAN ZONES

Figure 2-8 *Ocean temperatures vary from the Caribbean Sea to the White Cliffs of Dover to the polar regions. Notice the blue-green bacteria below the frozen surface of Lake Hoare in Antarctica.*

1500 meters, the temperature is about 4°C. So the temperature of most ocean water is just above freezing (0°C)!

The three ocean zones are not found in the polar regions. In the Arctic and Antarctic oceans, the surface waters are always very cold. The temperature changes only slightly as the depth increases.

Activity Bank

Sink or Swim—Is It Easier to Float in Cold Water or Hot?, p.167

2-2 Section Review

1. What does ocean water consist of?
2. What is salinity?
3. What three gases are most abundant in ocean water?
4. What are the three zones of the ocean? On what property of ocean water are these zones based?

Critical Thinking—*Applying Concepts*

5. Fish get the oxygen they need by removing it from water. Would you expect to find greater numbers of fish near the equator or in ocean areas farther north and south of the equator? Explain your answer. (*Hint:* Consider the effect of temperature on the amount of gases that can dissolve in water.)

2-3 The Ocean Floor

A description of the shape of the ocean floor—its characteristics and major features—is known as its topography. The topography of the ocean floor is different from the topography of the continents. The ocean floor has higher mountains, deeper canyons, and larger, flatter plains than the continents. The ocean floor also has more volcanoes than the continents. Earthquakes occur with greater frequency under the ocean than on the land. The rocks that form the ocean floor are very different from the rocks that form the crust of the continents. The crust of the Earth is much thinner under the ocean than under the continents.

Edges of the Continents

On a continent, there is a boundary where the land and the ocean meet. This boundary is called a **shoreline.** A shoreline marks the average position of sea level. It does not mark the end of the continent.

The edge of a continent extends into the ocean. The area where the underwater edge of a continent meets the ocean floor is called a **continental margin.** Although a continental margin forms part of the ocean floor, it is more a part of the land than it is a part of the ocean.

A continental margin generally consists of a continental shelf, a continental slope, and a continental rise. Sediments worn away from the land are deposited in these parts of a continental margin.

The relatively flat part of a continental margin that is covered by shallow ocean water is called a **continental shelf.** A continental shelf usually slopes very gently downward from the shoreline. In fact, it usually slopes less than 1.2 meters for every 100 meters from the shoreline.

The width of a continental shelf varies. Off the Atlantic coast, the continental shelf extends more than 200 kilometers into the ocean. Off the Arctic shore of Siberia, the continental shelf extends over 1200 kilometers into the ocean. Off the coast of southeastern Florida, there is almost no continental shelf.

Guide for Reading

Focus on these questions as you read.

▶ *What are the parts of a continental margin?*

▶ *What are some major features of the ocean floor?*

Figure 2-9 *An offshore oil rig drills for oil trapped beneath the ocean floor in the continental shelf.*

ACTIVITY READING

The Great Whale

Moby Dick is one of the greatest stories ever written in the English language. This tale of the sea and the whalers who sailed it describes a time when people made a living by hunting the great whales. You might enjoy reading this book written by Herman Melville and reporting on it to your class.

Figure 2–10 *In this illustration, you can see the major features of the ocean floor. What are some of these features?*

The best fishing areas of the ocean are found in waters over a continental shelf. Large mineral deposits, as well as large deposits of oil and natural gas are also found on a continental shelf. Because of the presence of these precious resources, many countries have extended their natural boundaries to include the continental shelf that lies off their shores.

At the edge of a continental shelf, the ocean floor plunges steeply 4 to 5 kilometers. This part of the continental margin is called a **continental slope.** A continental slope marks the boundary between the crust of the continent and the crust of the ocean floor. Separating a continental slope from the ocean floor is a **continental rise.** You can see the parts of a continental margin and other features of the ocean floor in Figure 2–10.

A continental rise is made of large amounts of sediments. These sediments include small pieces of rocks and the remains of plants and animals washed down from the continent and the continental slope. Sometimes the sediments are carried down the slope in masses of flowing water called **turbidity** (ter-BIHD-uh-tee) **currents.** A turbidity current is a flow of water that carries large amounts of sediments. A turbidity current is like an underwater avalanche.

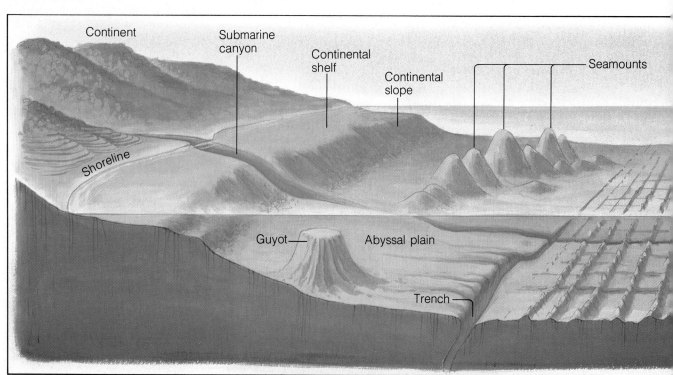

In many areas, **submarine canyons** cut through a continental shelf and slope. Submarine canyons are deep, V-shaped valleys that have been cut in rock. Some of the canyons are very deep indeed. For example, the Monterey Submarine Canyon off the coast of central California reaches depths of more than 2000 meters. It is actually deeper than the Grand Canyon!

Many scientists believe that submarine canyons are formed by powerful turbidity currents. Submarine canyons may also be caused by earthquakes or other movements that occur on a continental slope. Scientists still have much to learn about the origin and nature of submarine canyons.

Features of the Ocean Floor

Scientists have identified several major features of the ocean floor. (The ocean floor is also called the ocean basin.) Refer back to Figure 2–10 as you read about these features.

ABYSSAL PLAINS Large flat areas on the ocean floor are called **abyssal** (uh-BIHS-uhl) **plains.** The abyssal plains are larger in the Atlantic and Indian oceans than in the Pacific Ocean. Scientists believe

Figure 2–11 *These divers are exploring a submarine canyon in the continental shelf. How are submarine canyons formed?*

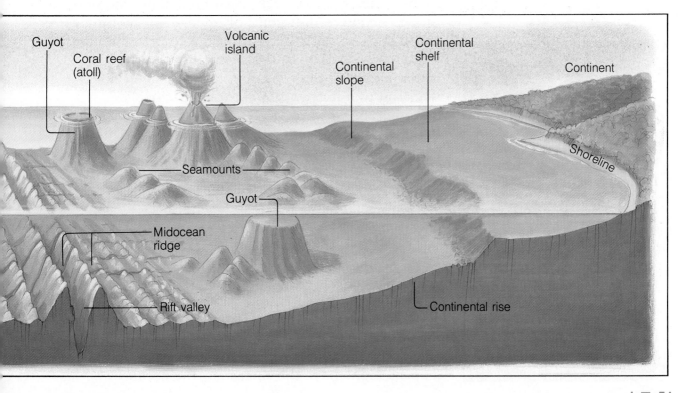

Figure 2–12 *The submersible* Alvin *searches for unusual organisms in the sediments covering the abyssal plains.*

that two reasons account for the difference in the size of these abyssal plains.

First, the world's greatest rivers flow directly or indirectly into the Atlantic and Indian oceans. These rivers include the Mississippi, Congo, Nile, and Amazon, which flow into the Atlantic Ocean, and the Ganges and Indus rivers which flow directly into the Indian Ocean. These major rivers, and many smaller ones, deposit large amounts of sediments on the abyssal plains.

Second, the floor of the Pacific Ocean contains a number of deep cracks along the edges of the continents. These long, narrow cracks trap sediments that are carried down a continental slope.

Deep-sea drilling operations and sound-wave detection equipment have shown that the sediments of the abyssal plains close to continents consist of thick layers of mud, sand, and silt. Farther out on the abyssal plains, some of the sediments contain the remains of tiny organisms. These organisms are so small they can be seen only with the aid of a microscope. They form a sediment called ooze. Where ocean life is not abundant, the floor of the ocean is covered with a sediment called red clay. Red clay is made of sediments carried to the oceans by rivers.

SEAMOUNTS AND GUYOTS Scattered along the floor of the ocean are thousands of underwater mountains called **seamounts.** Seamounts are volcanic mountains that rise more than 1000 meters above the surrounding ocean floor. Seamounts have steep sides that lead to a narrow summit (or top). To date, oceanographers have located more than 1000 seamounts. They expect to find thousands more in the future as more ocean areas are explored. Many more seamounts have been found in the Pacific Ocean than in either the Atlantic or the Indian Ocean.

Some seamounts reach above the surface of the ocean to form islands. The Azores and the Ascension Islands in the Atlantic Ocean are examples of volcanic islands. Perhaps the most dramatic and familiar volcanic islands are the Hawaiian Islands in the Pacific Ocean. The island of Hawaii is the top of a great volcano that rises more than 9600 meters from the ocean floor. It is the highest mountain on Earth when measured from its base on the ocean floor to its peak high above the surface of the ocean.

ACTIVITY

THINKING

Strolling Under the Seas

Imagine that all the water has been drained from all the oceans on Earth. Every feature once hidden under the waves is now seen easily. You and a friend decide to take a hike across the dry ocean floor. Choose a starting point and a destination. In a report, describe the features of the ocean floor you observe on your trip.

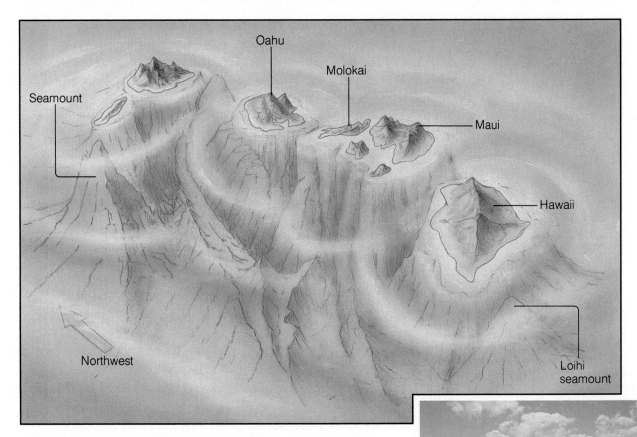

Figure 2-13 *The Hawaiian island of Kauai is the top of a seamount that extends above the ocean's surface (bottom). The age of the Hawaiian Islands increases as you travel toward the northwest. Loihi Seamount, off the coast of Hawaii, is slowly growing taller. Loihi will eventually become the newest Hawaiian island (top).*

During the mid-1940s, scientists discovered that many seamounts do not rise to a peak. Instead they have a flat top. These flat-topped seamounts are called **guyots** (gee-OHZ). Scientists believe that the flat tops are the result of wave erosion. Waves broke apart the tops of seamounts that once were at sea level. The flattened volcanic seamounts were later submerged.

TRENCHES The deepest parts of the ocean are not in the middle of the ocean floor. The greatest depths are found in **trenches** along the edges of the ocean floor. Trenches are long, narrow crevices (or cracks) that can be more than 11,000 meters deep.

The Pacific Ocean has more trenches than the other oceans. The Mariana Trench in the Pacific Ocean contains the deepest spot known on the Earth. This spot is called Challenger Deep. Challenger Deep is more than 11,000 meters deep. To

MAJOR OCEAN TRENCHES	
Trench	Depth (meters)
Pacific Ocean	
Aleutian	8100
Kurile	10,542
Japan	9810
Mariana (Challenger Deep)	11,034
Philippine	10,497
Tonga	10,882
Kermadec	10,800
Peru-Chile	8055
Mindanao	10,030
Atlantic Ocean	
Puerto Rico	8648
South Sandwich	8400

Figure 2–14 *Ocean trenches are the deepest parts of the ocean floor. Which ocean, the Atlantic or Pacific, has the most trenches?*

give you some idea of the depth of Challenger Deep, consider this: The Empire State Building in New York is about 430 meters tall. It would take a stack of 26 Empire State Buildings to break the ocean surface from the bottom of Challenger Deep!

MIDOCEAN RIDGES Some of the largest mountain ranges on Earth are located under the oceans. These mountain ranges are called **midocean ridges.** They form an almost continuous mountain belt that extends from the Arctic Ocean, down through the middle of the Atlantic Ocean, around Africa into the Indian Ocean, and then across the Pacific Ocean north to North America. In the Atlantic Ocean, the mountain belt is called the Mid-Atlantic Ridge. In the Pacific Ocean, the mountain belt is called the Pacific-Antarctic Ridge or East Pacific Rise or Ridge.

The midocean ridges are unlike any mountain ranges on land. Why? Mountain ranges on land are formed when the Earth's crust folds and is squeezed together. Midocean ridges are areas where molten (or hot liquid) material from deep within the Earth flows up to the surface. At the surface, the molten material cools and piles up to form new crust.

Figure 2–15 *This map shows the topography of the ocean floor.*

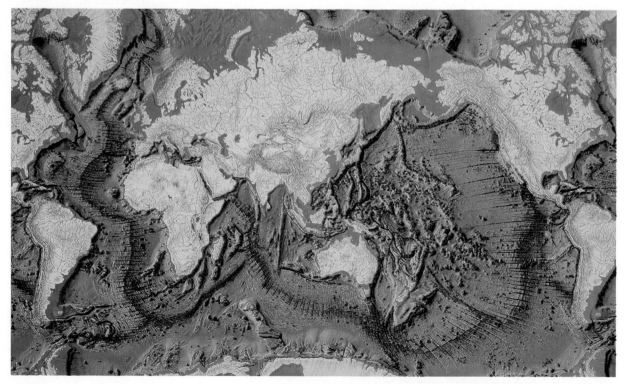

Figure 2-16 *This illustration shows a submarine above a rift valley surrounded by mountains that make up part of the oceanic ridge system. In the central part of the rift valley you can see molten rock that has cooled. This rock will eventually become new ocean floor (inset).*

Running along the middle of the midocean ridges between the rows of almost parallel mountains are deep crevices, or rift valleys. Rift valleys are about 25 to 50 kilometers wide and 1 to 2 kilometers below the bases of the surrounding midocean ridges. Rift valleys are regions of great earthquake and volcanic activity. In fact, rift valleys may mark the center of the areas where new crust is formed. Scientists have learned about changes in the Earth's crust by studying the rocks in and around the midocean ridges. Why do you think this is so?

REEFS Sometimes unusual-looking volcanic islands can be seen in tropical waters near a continental shelf. Surrounding these islands offshore are large masses and ridges of limestone rocks. The limestone structures contain the shells of animals and are called **coral reefs.** Because the reef-building organisms cannot survive in waters colder than 18°C, reefs are found only in tropical waters. Reefs are found in the warmer parts of the Pacific Ocean and in the Caribbean Sea. The organisms that build reefs also cannot live in deep water. They need sunlight to make their hard limestone skeletons. Not enough sunlight for these organisms to survive penetrates water deeper than 55 meters.

There are three types of coral reefs. One type is called **fringing reefs.** Fringing reefs are coral reefs that touch the shoreline of a volcanic island. Fringing reefs are generally less than 30 meters; however, some may be several hundred meters wide.

ACTIVITY
DOING

Ocean Floor Model

1. Use some paper-mâché, plaster of Paris, or modeling clay to construct a model of the ocean floor. Use Figures 2–10 and 2–15 to help you construct your model.

2. Label each feature in your model.

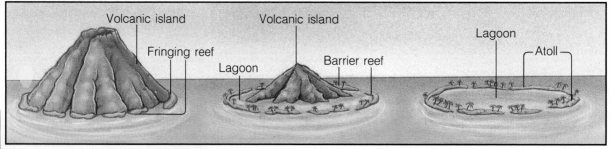

Volcanic island

Fringing reef

Volcanic island

Lagoon

Barrier reef

Lagoon

Atoll

Figure 2–17 *The development of the three types of coral reefs is shown in the illustration. A barrier reef is separated from the shore by a lagoon (top photograph). An atoll surrounds only a lagoon because the island has been worn away and is no longer above the ocean surface (bottom photograph).*

Barrier reefs are another type of coral reef. Barrier reefs are separated from the shore by an area of shallow water called a lagoon. Barrier reefs are generally larger than fringing reefs. And the islands that barrier reefs surround usually have sunk farther into the ocean than the islands that fringing reefs surround. The largest barrier reef on Earth is the Great Barrier Reef of Australia. It is about 2300 kilometers long and ranges from 40 to 320 kilometers wide. The Great Barrier Reef is rich in many kinds of animal and plant life.

The third type of coral reef can be found farther out in the ocean. It is a ring of coral reefs called an **atoll.** An atoll surrounds an island that has been worn away and has sunk beneath the surface of the ocean. Figure 2–17 shows the three types of coral reefs.

2–3 Section Review

1. What is the continental margin? Describe the parts of a continental margin.
2. Identify five major features of the ocean floor.
3. What are three types of coral reefs?

Connection—*Literature*

4. A famous science fiction writer once said that "... good science fiction must also be good science." In a new science fiction movie, a giant sea monster lives in a coral reef off the coast of Maine near the Canadian border. During the day, the monster terrorizes the local population, devouring pets and people. At night it returns to the safety of its reef. Is this plot good science fiction? Explain your answer.

2–4 Ocean Life Zones

Guide for Reading

Focus on these questions as you read.

▶ What are the three major groups of animals and plants in the ocean?

▶ What are the three major life zones in the ocean?

A visit to a public aquarium will convince you that a great variety of life exists in the ocean. But even the most well-stocked aquarium is home to relatively few kinds of fishes and plants. People who visit a real coral reef, for example, swim away amazed at the colors, shapes, and variety of the fishes that inhabit the reef.

The animal and plant life found in the ocean is affected by several factors. One factor is the amount of sunlight that penetrates the ocean. Another factor is the temperature of the water. Because there is less sunlight deep in the ocean, the temperature is much lower. So more plants and animals are found in the upper layers of the ocean and near the shoreline than in the deeper layers. Another factor that affects ocean life is water pressure. Water pressure increases as depth increases. Do you know why? With increasing depth, the amount of water pushing down from above increases. This increases the pressure. Organisms that live deep in the ocean must be able to withstand great pressure.

The animals and plants in the ocean can be classified into three major groups according to their habits and the depth of the water in which they live. The largest group of animals and plants is called **plankton** (PLANGK-tuhn). Plankton float at or near the surface of the ocean where sunlight penetrates. Near the shore, they live at depths of about 1 meter. In the open ocean, they can be found at depths of up to 200 meters.

Most plankton are very small. In fact, many forms are microscopic. These organisms drift with the currents and tides of the ocean. Tiny shrimplike organisms and various forms of algae are all plankton. Plankton are the main food for many larger organisms, including the largest organisms on Earth—whales. Certain kinds of whales strain plankton from the water. It is interesting to note that the throat of some of the largest whales is so small that they cannot swallow food larger than a fifty-cent piece!

Forms of ocean life that swim are called **nekton** (NEHK-ton). Whales, seals, dolphins, squid, octopuses, barracudas, and other fishes are all nekton.

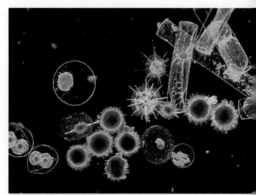

Figure 2–18 *Microscopic plankton (top) are the main source of food for many large sea creatures. The Southern right whale uses its strainerlike mouth to filter plankton from ocean water. Can you imagine how many plankton it must take to satisfy this whale's appetite?*

Figure 2–19 *Among the most-feared nekton, or forms of life that swim, are the sharks. Here you see the dangerous great white shark (left), the huge and harmless whale shark (top right), and the bottom-dwelling leopard shark (bottom right).*

Because they can swim, nekton are able to actively search for food and avoid predators. Predators are organisms that eat other organisms. The organisms that get eaten are called prey. Some types of sharks are feared predators in the ocean; other fish are their prey.

Nekton can be found at all levels of the ocean. Some swim near the ocean surface, others along the bottom. Some are found in the deepest parts of the ocean. Because they can swim, nekton can move from one part of the ocean to another. But they remain in areas where conditions are most favorable.

Organisms that live on the ocean floor are called **benthos** (BEHN-thahs). Some benthos are plants that grow on the ocean floor in shallow waters. Plants are able to survive in water only where sunlight penetrates. Other benthos are animals such as barnacles, oysters, crabs, and starfish. Many benthos, such as sea anemones, attach themselves to the ocean floor. Others live in shore areas. A few kinds live on the ocean floor in the deepest parts of the ocean.

Figure 2–20 *The sea anemone's "tentacles" carry stinging cells that enable it to capture unsuspecting fish. The clownfish swimming between the tentacles is immune to the anemone's poison. It helps attract other fish to the anemone. How does this unusual behavior help the clownfish survive?*

Intertidal Zone

As you just read, there are three major groups of ocean life. There are also three major environments, or life zones, in the ocean. **The classification of the ocean into life zones is based on the conditions in the ocean—conditions that vary widely.** There are

Figure 2-21 *The intertidal zone lies between the low- and high-tide lines. Organisms that live in the intertidal zone include starfish (inset), giant limpets (inset), clams (top right), barnacles (center), and sea anemones (bottom right).*

shallow beach areas that dry out twice a day and then become wet again. There are ocean depths where no ray of sunlight ever reaches and where the temperature stays a few degrees above freezing all year round. And in between these extremes is the open ocean with a range of environments at different depths. Scientists know a great deal about these areas, but much of the ocean still remains an unexplored frontier.

The region that lies between the low– and high–tide lines is the **intertidal zone.** This region is the most changeable zone in the ocean. Sometimes it is ocean. Sometimes it is dry land. These changes occur

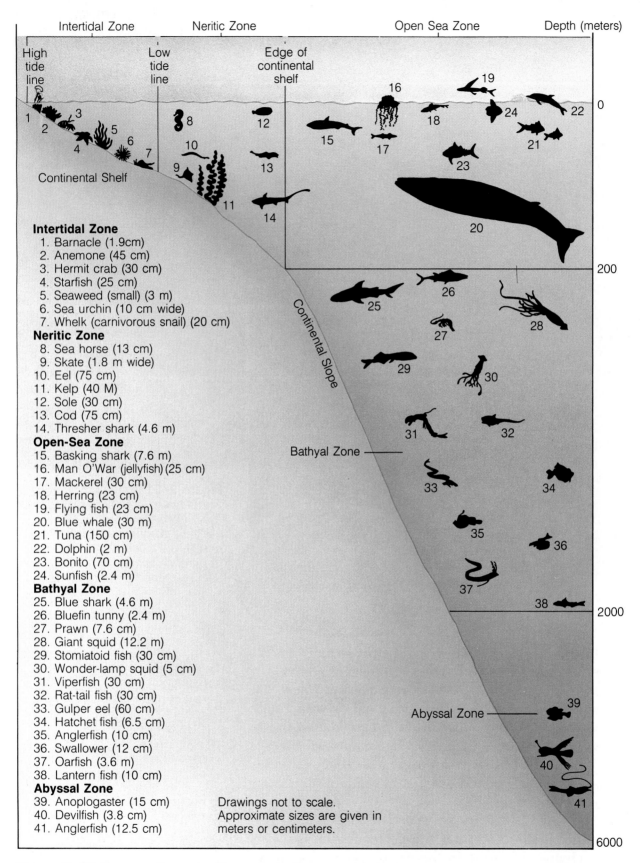

Intertidal Zone · Neritic Zone · Open Sea Zone · Depth (meters)

High tide line · Low tide line · Edge of continental shelf

Continental Shelf

Continental Slope

Bathyal Zone

Abyssal Zone

0

200

2000

6000

Intertidal Zone
1. Barnacle (1.9cm)
2. Anemone (45 cm)
3. Hermit crab (30 cm)
4. Starfish (25 cm)
5. Seaweed (small) (3 m)
6. Sea urchin (10 cm wide)
7. Whelk (carnivorous snail) (20 cm)

Neritic Zone
8. Sea horse (13 cm)
9. Skate (1.8 m wide)
10. Eel (75 cm)
11. Kelp (40 M)
12. Sole (30 cm)
13. Cod (75 cm)
14. Thresher shark (4.6 m)

Open-Sea Zone
15. Basking shark (7.6 m)
16. Man O'War (jellyfish) (25 cm)
17. Mackerel (30 cm)
18. Herring (23 cm)
19. Flying fish (23 cm)
20. Blue whale (30 m)
21. Tuna (150 cm)
22. Dolphin (2 m)
23. Bonito (70 cm)
24. Sunfish (2.4 m)

Bathyal Zone
25. Blue shark (4.6 m)
26. Bluefin tunny (2.4 m)
27. Prawn (7.6 cm)
28. Giant squid (12.2 m)
29. Stomiatoid fish (30 cm)
30. Wonder-lamp squid (5 cm)
31. Viperfish (30 cm)
32. Rat-tail fish (30 cm)
33. Gulper eel (60 cm)
34. Hatchet fish (6.5 cm)
35. Anglerfish (10 cm)
36. Swallower (12 cm)
37. Oarfish (3.6 m)
38. Lantern fish (10 cm)

Abyssal Zone
39. Anoplogaster (15 cm)
40. Devilfish (3.8 cm)
41. Anglerfish (12.5 cm)

Drawings not to scale.
Approximate sizes are given in meters or centimeters.

Figure 2-22 *Here are the major life zones in the ocean, their depths, and some of the living things usually found in these zones. Above what depth is most ocean life found?*

Figure 2–23 *Mandarin, or psychedelic, fish (left) and the highly venomous lion fish (right) are but two of the many types of fishes that inhabit Earth's oceans.*

twice a day as the ocean surges up the shore at high tide and retreats at low tide. It is difficult for living things to survive in the intertidal zone. The tides and the waves breaking along the shore constantly move materials in this zone. Because the tide rises and falls, organisms must be able to live without water some of the time.

Some of the organisms that live in the intertidal zone are anemones, crabs, clams, mussels, and plants such as certain kinds of seaweeds. To keep from being washed out to sea, many of these organisms attach themselves to sand and rocks. Others, such as certain worms and some kinds of shellfish, burrow into the wet sand for protection.

Neritic Zone

The **neritic** (nee-RIHT-ihk) **zone** extends from the low-tide line to the edge of a continental shelf. This zone extends to a depth of about 200 meters.

The neritic zone receives plenty of sunlight. The water pressure is low and the temperature remains fairly constant. Here the ocean floor is covered with seaweed. Many different animals and plants live in this zone, including plankton, nekton, and benthos. In fact, the neritic zone is richer in life than any other ocean zone. Most of the world's great fishing areas are within this zone. Fish, clams, snails, some types of whales, and lobsters are but a few of the kinds of organisms that live in the neritic zone. This

Figure 2–24 *This California spiny lobster searching for food at night is among the many interesting creatures in the neritic zone.*

ACTIVITY

DOING

Fish for the Table

Visit a supermarket or a fish market. List the different foods available that come from the ocean. Answer the following questions about the foods you listed:

1. Which foods are plankton? Nekton? Benthos?

2. From which ocean-life zone did each food come?

3. Where did the store obtain each food?

4. Which foods are sold fresh? Which are sold frozen?

5. Which foods have you eaten?

zone is the source of much of the seafood people eat. The neritic zone ends where there is too little sunlight for seaweed to grow.

Open-Ocean Zones

There are two open-ocean zones. The first is the **bathyal** (BAHTH-ee-uhl) **zone.** It begins at a continental slope and extends down about 2000 meters. Sunlight is not able to penetrate to the bottom of this zone. Many forms of nekton live in the bathyal zone, including squid, octopus, and large whales. Because there is little sunlight in the lower parts, plants do not grow near the bottom of this zone.

At a depth of about 2000 meters, the **abyssal zone** begins. This is the second open-ocean zone. The abyssal zone extends to an average depth of 6000 meters. This zone covers the large, flat plains of the ocean. No sunlight is able to penetrate to this zone. Thus little food is available. The water pressure is very great. What do you think the temperatures are like in the abyssal zone?

Even with extremely harsh conditions, life exists in the abyssal zone. Most of the animals that live here are small. Many are quite strange looking. Look again at the anoplogaster shown in the chapter opener. Some of the animals that live in this zone are able to make their own light.

Figure 2–25 *Organisms that live in the open-ocean zone include deep-sea anglerfish (top left), hatchet fish (bottom left), and krill (right).*

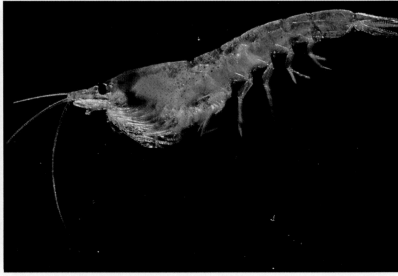

1. What are the three major groups of ocean life?
2. What are some factors that affect ocean life?
3. Describe the three major ocean life zones.
4. Which zone contains the greatest variety of ocean life? Why?

Critical Thinking—*Applying Concepts*
5. Most commercial fishing occurs near the ocean surface. Why would fishing in extremely deep water prove to be unsuccessful?

2–5 Mapping the Ocean Floor

The oceans have been called the last great unexplored places on Earth. In fact, we probably know more about some of our neighbors in outer space than we do about the waters that make up almost 71 percent of our planet.

In 1872, the first expedition to explore the ocean began when the *Challenger* sailed from England. Equipped for ocean exploration, the *Challenger* remained at sea for $3\frac{1}{2}$ years. Scientists aboard the *Challenger* used wire to measure ocean depth. They used nets attached to heavy ropes to collect animals and plants from the ocean floor. Organisms that had

Guide for Reading

Focus on this question as you read.

▶ *How is the ocean floor mapped?*

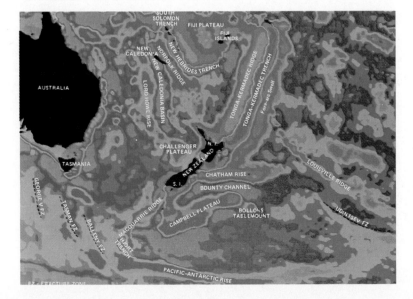

Figure 2–26 *This computerized geologic map of the southwest Pacific sea floor was constructed from data collected by a NASA satellite orbiting the Earth.*

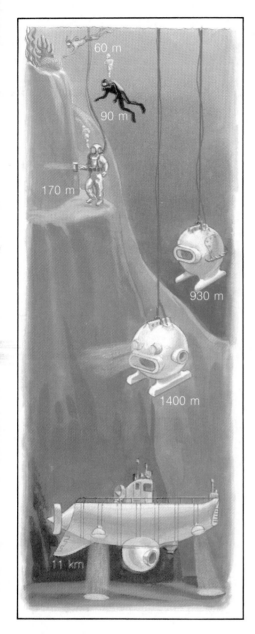

Figure 2–27 *Different instruments are used to explore the ocean. The type of instrument used is determined by the ocean depth. To what depth can a person descend without special breathing equipment?*

60 m

90 m

170 m

930 m

1400 m

11 km

long remained undisturbed—free from the probing eyes of humans—were brought to the surface. Special thermometers enabled the scientists to record deep-ocean temperatures. And samples of ocean water were collected in special bottles.

Today oceanographers have many modern instruments to aid them in the exploration of the oceans. Underwater cameras provide pictures of the ocean floor. Devices called corers bring up samples of mud and sand from the ocean bottom. And a variety of vehicles, including bathyspheres, bathyscaphs, and other submersibles, are able to dive deep under the surface to explore the ocean depths.

One of the most important goals of oceanographers is to map the ocean floor. **Mapping the ocean floor can only be done by indirect methods, such as echo sounding, radar, sonar, and seismographic surveys.** All of these methods are based on the same principle: Energy waves, such as sound waves, sent down to the ocean surface are reflected from (bounce off) the ocean floor and return to the surface, where they are recorded. Knowing the speed of sound in water, which is about 1500 meters per second, and the time it takes sound waves to make a round trip, oceanographers can determine the ocean depth at any location along the ocean floor.

The most complete picture of the ocean floor has been pieced together from information gathered by *Seasat*, a scientific satellite launched in 1978. From the 8 billion readings radioed back by *Seasat*, scientists have created the most accurate map yet.

2–5 Section Review

1. Name three instruments used by oceanographers today to explore the ocean. How do these instruments compare with ones used in the earliest expeditions?
2. What two pieces of information are needed to map the ocean depth using sonar?

Connection—*You and Your World*

3. Even though the oceans are one of the grandest features of Planet Earth, we know relatively little about them. What are some reasons to explain this lack of knowledge?

2–6 Motions of the Ocean

Ocean water never stops moving. **There are three basic motions of ocean water: the up and down movement of waves, the steady movement of ocean currents, and the rise and fall of ocean water in tides.** In this section you will read more about each of these ocean movements.

Waves

Waves are pulses of energy that move through the ocean. Waves are set in motion by winds, earthquakes, and the gravitational pull of the moon. The most common source of energy for waves, however, is wind blowing across the surface of the ocean.

Have you ever observed ocean waves—first far out at sea and then closer to shore? If not, perhaps you have seen pictures of them. Ocean waves begin as wind-stirred ripples on the surface of the water. As more energy is transferred from wind to water, the waves formed look like great forward surges of rapidly moving water. But the water is not moving forward at all! Only energy moves forward through the water, producing one wave after another. The energy is passed from one particle of water to another. But the particles of water themselves remain in relatively the same positions.

Wave energy is not only passed forward from one water particle to another, it is also passed downward from particle to particle. With increasing depth, the motion of the particles decreases. At a certain depth, motion stops. In deep water, there are no waves except for those caused by tides and earthquakes.

The height of surface waves depends upon three different factors. Do you know what they are? These factors are the wind's speed, the length of time the wind blows, and the distance the wind blows over the water. As each of these factors increases, the height of a wave increases. And some waves can become really huge. The largest surface wave ever measured in the middle of any ocean occurred in the North Pacific on February 7, 1933. At that time, a wind storm was sweeping over a stretch of water thousands of kilometers long. A ship in the United States Navy, the *U.S.S. Ramapo,* was plowing through

Figure 2–28 *Waves are set in motion as energy is transferred from wind to water. The wave pulses of energy are passed forward from particle to particle, as well as downward from particle to particle. Notice that it is not the water that is moving forward, but the pulse of energy.*

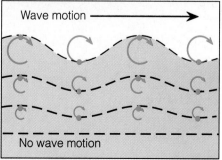

Wave motion ⟶

No wave motion

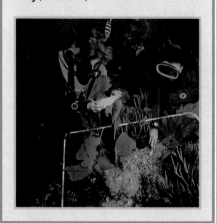
FACTORS THAT AFFECT THE HEIGHT OF SURFACE WAVES

Wind Speed (m/sec)	Length of Time Wind Blows (hr)	Distance Wind Blows Over Water (km)	Average Height of Wave (m)
5.1	2.4	18.5	0.27
10.2	10.0	140.0	1.5
15.3	23.0	520.0	4.1
20.4	42.0	1320.0	8.5
25.5	69.0	2570.0	14.8

Figure 2–29 *The factors that affect the height of surface waves are shown in this chart. What happens to the height of a wave as the wind speed increases?*

the sea when its officers spotted and measured a gigantic wave. It was at least 34 meters high! Such a wave would rise above a ten-story apartment house.

WAVE CHARACTERISTICS Ocean waves, like all other waves, have several characteristics. The highest point of a wave is called the **crest.** The lowest point of a wave is called the **trough** (TRAWF). The horizontal distance between two consecutive (one after the other) crests or two consecutive troughs is called the **wavelength.** The vertical distance between a crest and a trough is called the wave height. Waves have various wavelengths and wave heights. The basic characteristics of waves are shown in Figure 2–30.

Figure 2–30 *Characteristics of ocean waves are shown in this diagram. What is the distance between two consecutive crests called? What is the lowest point of a wave called?*

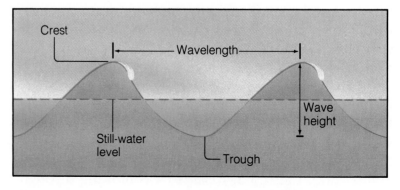

The amount of time it takes consecutive crests or troughs to pass a given point is called the wave period. The number of crests or troughs passing a given point in a certain wave period is called the wave frequency. What is the relationship between wavelength and wave frequency?

Out in the open ocean, waves stay about the same distance apart for thousands of kilometers. So wavelength is usually constant. These waves are called swells. Swells are long, wide waves that are not very high.

But waves change as they approach the shore. They slow down, and they get closer and closer together. Their wavelength decreases and their wave height increases. They finally crash forward as breakers and surge onto the shore. This surging water is called the surf.

The water then flows back toward the ocean. Bits of seaweed, sand, and pebbles are pulled back by the retreating water. This retreating water is called an undertow. Undertows can be quite strong. Occasionally, they can be strong enough to pose danger to swimmers, pulling them farther out into the ocean and under the water. Undertows can also extend for several kilometers offshore.

TSUNAMIS Some ocean waves are caused by earthquakes. These waves are called **tsunamis** (tsoo-NAH-meez). Tsunami is a Japanese word meaning "large wave in a harbor." Tsunamis are the highest ocean waves.

Figure 2–31 *The pattern of a swell as it reaches a sloping beach is shown in this diagram. What happens to the wavelength and the wave height as the wave nears the beach?*

Figure 2–32 *The power of a tsunami left this boat high and dry on the dock.*

Tsunamis have very long wavelengths and are very deep. They carry a huge amount of energy. As tsunamis slow down in shallow water, they pile closer and closer together. Their wave heights increase. The energy that was once spread throughout a great depth of water is now concentrated in much less water. This energy produces the tsunamis, which can reach heights of 35 meters or more when they strike the shore. To give you some idea of the imposing height of a tsunami, consider this: The average height of a building story is between 3 and 4 meters. So a 35-meter wave is about the height of a ten-story building!

As you might suspect, tsunamis can cause great damage and loss of life along coastal areas. One of the most famous groups of tsunamis was caused by the volcanic eruption of Krakatoa between Java and Sumatra in 1883. Nine tsunamis that rose up to 40 meters high hit along the Java coast. Nothing was left of the coastal towns and about 36,000 people died.

Currents

You can easily see water moving on the surface of the ocean in the form of waves. But it is not only water on the surface that moves. Water below the surface also has motion. This water moves in streams called currents. Some currents are so large—up to several thousand kilometers long—that they are better described as "rivers" in the ocean. In fact, the mighty Mississippi River can be considered a mere brook when compared with the largest of the ocean currents. But long or short, all ocean currents are caused by the same two factors: wind patterns and differences in water density.

SURFACE CURRENTS Currents caused mainly by wind patterns are called **surface currents.** These currents usually have a depth of several hundred meters. Some surface currents are warm-water currents, others are cold-water currents. The temperature of a current depends upon where the current originates. A warm current begins in a warm area. A cold current begins in a cold area.

Surface currents that travel thousands of kilometers are called long-distance surface currents. The

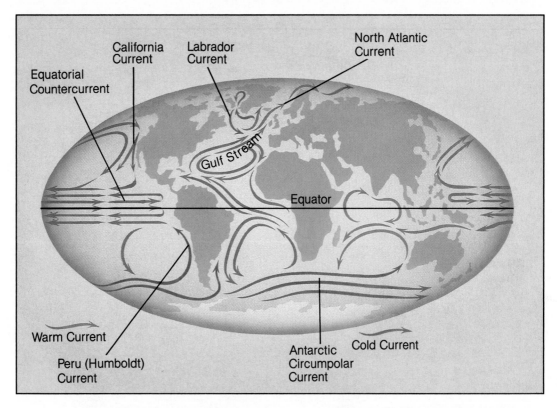

Figure 2–33 *This map shows the directions of flow of the major long-distance surface currents. Is the Gulf Stream a warm or a cold current?*

Gulf Stream is a well-known long-distance surface current. It is about 150 kilometers wide and may reach a depth of about 1000 meters. It carries warm water from the southern tip of Florida north along the eastern coast of the United States. It moves along at speeds greater than 1.5 meters per second. And more than 150 million cubic meters of water may pass a given point each second!

Figure 2–33 shows the major warm and cold surface currents of the world and the general directions in which they flow. Because all the oceans are connected, these ocean currents form a continuous worldwide pattern of water circulation.

You will notice from Figure 2–33 that the water in each ocean moves in a large, almost circular pattern. In the Northern Hemisphere, the currents move clockwise, or the same way the hands of a clock move. In the Southern Hemisphere, the currents move counterclockwise, or in the opposite direction. These motions correspond to the direction of wind circulation in each hemisphere.

As you might expect, surface currents that move over short distances are called short-distance surface currents. These currents usually are found near a shoreline where waves hit at an angle. When the

Figure 2–34 *Two surface currents converge, or come together, in the Atlantic Ocean near Bermuda.*

I ■ 69

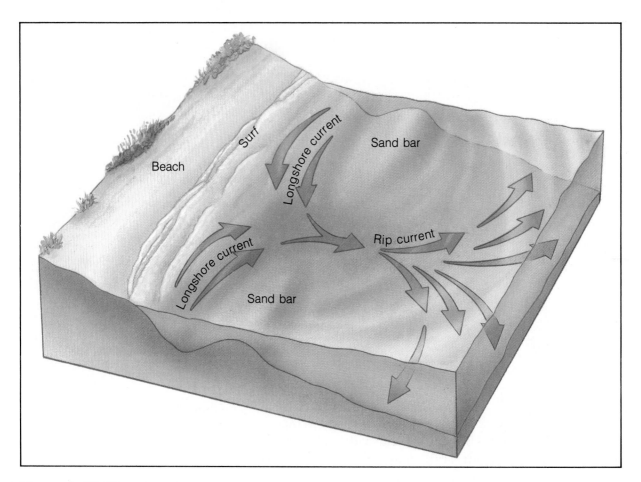

Figure 2–35 *When longshore currents cut through a sand bar, a rip current is formed.*

waves hit the shoreline, the water turns and produces currents that move parallel to the shoreline. These streams of water are called longshore currents.

As longshore currents move parallel to the shoreline, they pick up large quantities of material, such as sand from the beach. The sand is deposited in water close to the shoreline. A long, underwater pile of sand called a sand bar builds up.

Longshore currents can become trapped on the shoreline side of a sand bar. These currents may eventually cut an opening in the sandbar. The currents then return to the ocean in a powerful narrow flow called a rip current. A rip current is a type of undertow.

DEEP CURRENTS Some currents are caused mainly by differences in the density of water deep in the ocean. Such currents are called **deep currents.** The density, which you can think of as the heaviness of water, is affected by temperature and salinity. (Density is actually defined as mass per unit volume of a substance.) Cold water is more dense than warm water. And the saltier water is, the more dense it is. For example, cold dense water flowing from the polar regions moves downward under less dense warm water found in areas away from the poles.

Cameras lowered to the ocean floor have photographed evidence of powerful deep currents. The photograph in Figure 2–36 shows ripples carved into the sand of the ocean floor. In places on the floor, heavy clay has been piled into small dunes, as if shaped by winds. These "winds," scientists conclude, must be very strong ocean currents.

Most deep currents flow in the opposite direction from surface currents. For example, in the summer the Mediterranean Sea loses more water by evaporation than it gets back as rain. The salinity and density of the Mediterranean Sea increase. As a result, deep currents of dense water flow from the Mediterranean into the Atlantic Ocean. At the same time, the less salty and thus less dense water of the Atlantic Ocean flows into the Mediterranean at the water's surface.

The densest ocean water on Earth lies off the coast of Antarctica. This dense, cold Antarctic water sinks to the ocean floor and tends to flow north through the world's oceans. These deep Antarctic currents travel for thousands of kilometers. At the same time, warm surface currents near the equator tend to flow south toward Antarctica.

As the deep Antarctic currents come close to land, the ocean floor rises, forcing these cold currents upward. The rising of deep cold currents to the ocean surface is called **upwelling.** Upwelling is very important because the rising currents carry with them rich foodstuffs that have drifted down to the ocean floor. The foodstuffs are usually the remains of dead animals and plants. Wherever these deep currents rise, they turn the ocean into an area of plentiful ocean life. For example, deep currents move upward off the coasts of Peru and Chile. The nutrients they carry to the surface produce rich fishing grounds and important fishing industries in these areas.

Figure 2–36 *In this photograph you can see ripples carved into the ocean floor by a slow-moving deep current.*

Figure 2–37 *Areas of upwelling are important fishing areas because ocean life is plentiful. What factors cause upwelling?*

Figure 2–38 *The daily rise and fall of tides is magnificently evident at the Bay of Fundy in Canada.*

Figure 2–39 *Spring tides occur when the sun and the moon are in line with the Earth. Neap tides occur when the sun and the moon are at right angles to the Earth.*

Tides

Tides are the regular rise and fall of ocean water caused by the gravitational attraction among the Earth, moon, and sun. The Earth's gravity pulls on the moon. But the moon's gravity also pulls on the Earth, producing a bulging of the ocean. The ocean bulges in two places: on the side of the Earth that faces the moon, and on the side of the Earth that faces away from the moon. Both bulges cause a high tide, or rising of ocean water, on nearby shorelines.

At the same time that the high tides occur, low tides occur between the two bulges. Observations show that at most places on Earth there are two high tides and two low tides every 24 hours.

Some high tides are higher than other high tides. For example, when the moon is at its full- and new-moon phases, the Earth has higher tides than at other times. These higher tides are called spring tides. Spring tides occur when the sun and the moon are in line with the Earth (which is the arrangement of the sun, moon, and Earth during full-moon and new moon phases). The increased gravitational effect due to the sun's gravity causes the ocean bulges to become even larger than usual.

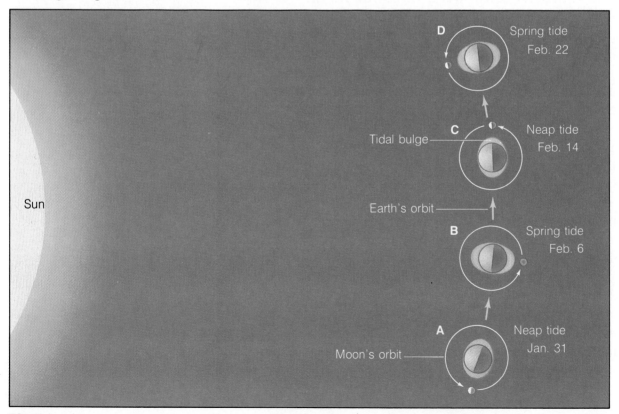

When the moon is at its first- and last-quarter phases, its gravitational pull on the oceans is partially canceled by the gravitational pull of the sun. High tides that are lower than usual result. These minimum high tides are called neap tides. What is the position of the sun and moon with respect to each other during neap tides?

2–6 Section Review

1. What are the three basic motions of the ocean?
2. What are four characteristics of a wave?
3. What are currents? What is the difference between surface currents and deep currents?
4. What are tides? What causes them?

Critical Thinking—*Relating Cause and Effect*
5. For maximum excitement, a surfer wants to find the highest waves possible. In what ocean would the surfer have the best chance of finding enormous waves? Why?

The Moon's Attraction

Tide forecasts for each month are usually given in the newspaper on the first day of the month. You can also find tide forecasts in the *Farmer's Almanac.*

Use the information to plot a graph of daily high- and low-tide heights for the month. There are two high and two low tides given for each day. Plot only the heights that occur earlier in the day.

What is the relationship of the phases of the moon to the tide heights?

CONNECTIONS

The Sound of the Surf

Waves are beautiful to watch and thrilling to listen to. Even the smallest waves do not creep silently onto a beach. Instead they break with a gentle sigh. And when large waves break on shore, the crashing sounds are quite impressive. Did you ever wonder why waves make noise when they roll onto shore? The explanation may surprise you.

The answer to this question is as near as the bubble gum in your mouth. When you blow a bubble, you trap air in the gum. When the bubble breaks, it makes a popping sound. Breaking bubbles of trapped air also cause a sound when waves break. Ocean water picks up tiny bubbles of air, bubbles that become trapped within the water. When waves crash on the shore, the tiny air bubbles in the waves break. The characteristic sound of waves is produced. Keep this in mind, however. Even though there is a sound scientific reason that explains the *physics* of the noise, waves are still beautiful to look at and still wonderful to listen to.

Laboratory Investigation

The Effect of Water Depth on Sediments

Problem

To determine the effects that differences in water depth have on the settling of sediments.

Materials *(per group)*

plastic tubes of different lengths that contain sediment samples and salt water

Procedure

1. Obtain a plastic tube from your teacher.
2. Make sure that both ends of the tube are securely capped.

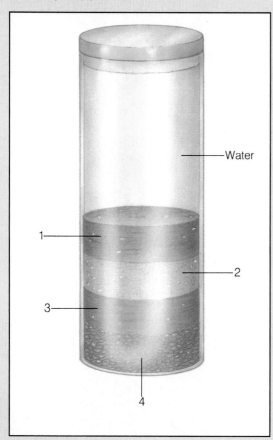

3. Hold the tube by both ends and gently tip it back and forth until the sediments in the tube are thoroughly mixed throughout the water.
4. Set the tube in an upright position in a place where it will not be disturbed.
5. Repeat steps 1 through 4 for each of the remaining tubes.
6. Carefully observe the sediments in each tube.

Observations

1. Make a detailed sketch to illustrate the heights of the different layers formed when the sediments in each tube settled.
2. What general statement can you make about the size of the sediment particles and the order in which each type of sediment settled in the tube?

Analysis and Conclusions

1. What effect does the length of the water column have on the number and types of sediment layers formed in each tube?
2. How are these tubes accurate models of what happens to sediments carried to the ocean?
3. What is the variable present in this investigation? What variables that may be present in the ocean are not tested in this investigation?
4. **On Your Own** Design an investigation to determine the effect of different amounts of salinity on the formation of sediment layers.

Study Guide

Summarizing Key Concepts

2–1 The World's Oceans

▲ The Atlantic, Pacific, and Indian oceans are the three major oceans.

2–2 Properties of Ocean Water

▲ Ocean water is a mixture of gases and solids dissolved in pure water.

▲ Ocean water is classified into three zones based on water temperature: surface zone, thermocline, and deep zone.

2–3 The Ocean Floor

▲ A continental margin consists of a continental shelf, a continental slope, and a continental rise.

▲ Major features of the ocean floor include, abyssal plains, seamounts, guyots, trenches, midocean ridges, rift valleys, and reefs.

2–4 Ocean Life Zones

▲ Ocean life forms are classified by habits and depth in which they live.

▲ The three major ocean life zones are the intertidal, neritic and open-ocean zones.

2–5 Mapping the Ocean Floor

▲ The ocean floor is mapped by echo sounding, radar, sonar, and seismographic surveys.

2–6 Motions of the Ocean

▲ Motions of the ocean include waves, currents, and tides.

▲ Waves have the following characteristics: crests, troughs, wavelength, wave height, wave period, and wave frequency.

▲ Surface currents are caused mainly by wind patterns; deep currents by differences in the density of ocean water.

▲ Tides are the regular rise and fall of ocean water caused by the gravitational attraction among the Earth, moon, and sun.

Reviewing Key Terms

Define each term in a complete sentence.

2–2 Properties of Ocean Water
oceanographer
salinity
surface zone
thermocline
deep zone

2–3 The Ocean Floor
shoreline
continental margin
continental shelf
continental slope
continental rise
turbidity current
submarine canyon
abyssal plain
seamounts
guyot
trench
midocean ridge
coral reef
fringing reef
barrier reef
atoll

2–4 Ocean Life Zones
plankton
nekton
benthos
intertidal zone
neritic zone
bathyal zone
abyssal zone

2–6 Motions of the Ocean
crest
trough
wavelength
tsunami
surface current
deep current
upwelling

Chapter Review

Content Review

Multiple Choice

Choose the letter of the answer that best completes each statement.

1. The three major oceans of the world are the Atlantic, Pacific, and
   a. Arctic.
   b. Indian.
   c. Mediterranean.
   d. Caribbean.

2. The amount of dissolved salts in ocean water is called
   a. salinity.
   b. turbidity.
   c. upwelling.
   d. current.

3. The zone in the ocean where the temperature changes rapidly is called the
   a. surface zone.
   b. benthos.
   c. tide zone.
   d. thermocline.

4. The amount of time it takes consecutive wave crests or troughs to pass a given point is called the
   a. wavelength.
   b. tsunami.
   c. wave height.
   d. frequency.

5. All ocean currents are caused by
   a. winds and earthquakes.
   b. volcanoes and tides.
   c. winds and water density.
   d. tides and water density.

6. The most common source of energy for surface waves is
   a. wind.
   b. earthquakes.
   c. tides.
   d. volcanoes.

7. The deepest parts of the ocean are found in long, narrow crevices called
   a. guyots.
   b. seamounts.
   c. reefs.
   d. trenches.

8. Organisms that live on the ocean floor are called
   a. nekton.
   b. plankton.
   c. diatoms.
   d. benthos.

9. The rising of deep cold currents to the ocean surface is called
   a. surfing.
   b. upwelling.
   c. mapping.
   d. reefing.

10. High tides that are higher than other high tides are called
    a. tsunamis.
    b. neap tides.
    c. spring tides.
    d. ebb tides.

True or False

If the statement is true, write "true." If it is false, change the underlined word or words to make the statement true.

1. The most abundant salt in the ocean is <u>magnesium bromide</u>.
2. The lowest point of a wave is called the <u>crest</u>.
3. The Gulf Stream is a <u>long-distance</u> surface current.
4. Tides are caused mainly by the gravitational attraction of <u>Jupiter</u>.
5. The relatively flat part of a continental margin covered by shallow water is called a <u>continental slope</u>.
6. <u>Spring tides</u> occur during the first- and last-quarter phases of the moon.

Concept Mapping

Complete the following concept map for Section 2–1. Refer to pages 16–17 to construct a concept map for the entire chapter.

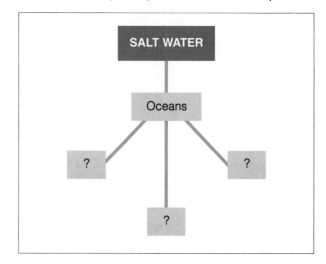

Concept Mastery

Discuss each of the following in a brief paragraph.

1. How do surface waves and deep waves differ?
2. How does the salinity of ocean water change with temperature?
3. Some of the largest animals in the oceans, (certain whales, for example) depend upon some of the smallest living organisms in the sea. Explain this statement.
4. List the three temperature zones of the ocean. Describe the physical conditions present in each zone.
5. Describe the topography of the ocean floor.
6. What are the three types of coral reefs? How are they alike? How are they different?

Critical Thinking and Problem Solving

Use the skills you have developed in this chapter to answer each of the following.

1. **Applying concepts** Many countries in the world extend their borders to a "two hundred mile limit" from shore. What are several reasons countries might impose this limit?
2. **Making inferences** Suppose conditions in the ocean changed and a major upwelling occurred off the coast of New York City. How would this change the life in the ocean in this area?
3. **Drawing conclusions** Suppose you were asked to design a special suit that would allow people to explore areas deep under the surface of the ocean. What are some important features the suit would need in order to help a diver survive?
4. **Applying concepts** Many legends tell of the appearance and disappearance of islands. Explain why such legends may be fact rather than fiction.
5. **Making calculations** Sound travels about 1500 meters per second in water. How deep would the ocean be if it took twenty seconds for a sound wave to return to the surface from the ocean bottom?
6. **Relating concepts** How do nekton organisms differ from benthos organisms?
7. **Identifying parts** The accompanying illustration shows a typical wave. Provide labels for the parts shown.
8. **Using the writing process** Suppose you and your family and friends lived in a huge glass bubble deep beneath the ocean waves. Write several pages in a diary to explain what life is like over a week's time.

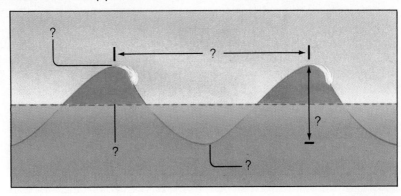

Earth's Fresh Water

Guide for Reading

After you read the following sections, you will be able to

3–1 Fresh Water on the Surface of the Earth

- Identify the sources of fresh water on the Earth's surface.
- Describe a watershed.

3–2 Fresh Water Beneath the Surface of the Earth

- Identify the sources of fresh water beneath the Earth's surface.
- Explain how fresh water forms caverns, stalactites, and stalagmites.

3–3 Water as a Solvent

- Describe how the polarity of water makes it a good solvent.
- List ways in which supplies of fresh water can be protected.

The newspaper headlines said it all. Water, a substance most people take for granted, was creating problems all over the country. In some places there was too little water, in other places too much.

A severe drought in the West had left hundreds of square kilometers of forest dry. Forest fires raged in these areas, causing heavy damage. Firefighters battled in vain to stem the fire's destructive path.

Meanwhile, heavy rains in some southern states had flooded rivers, lakes, and streams. Dams could no longer hold the huge quantities of water building up behind them. In several places, dams collapsed. Water and thick streams of mud buried land and homes under a heavy sheet of wet, brown dirt.

Perhaps you have never thought of water as the cause of such problems. To you, water is a natural resource you use every day to stay alive. In fact, more than 500 billion liters of water are used every day in the United States alone. Within the next 20 years, this staggering volume will probably double! Where does our supply of fresh water come from? Will there always be enough? In this chapter you will learn about the Earth's supply of fresh water, as well as the answers to these questions.

Journal *Activity*

You and Your World The average American family uses 760 liters of water a day. In some parts of the world, however, the average family uses 7 to 10 liters of water a day! Suppose your family's supply of water were limited to 10 liters a day. In your journal, make a list of the things you would use this water for. Make a list of the things you couldn't do.

◀ *Fresh water is one of the Earth's most important natural resources.*

Guide for Reading

*Focus on this question as
you read.*

▶ *What are the major
sources of fresh water on
the Earth's surface?*

3–1 Fresh Water on the Surface of the Earth

When you look at a photograph of Planet Earth taken from space, you can observe that water is one of the most abundant substances on Earth's surface. In fact, astronauts—whose views of Earth differ from those of most people—have described the Earth as the blue planet!

A casual glance at a world map might make you think that the Earth has an unending supply of fresh water—a supply that can meet the needs of living things forever. After all, the oceans cover more than 70 percent of the Earth's surface. Actually, about 97 percent of all the water on Earth is found in the oceans. But most of the ocean water cannot be used by living things because it contains salt. The salt would have to be removed before ocean water could be used.

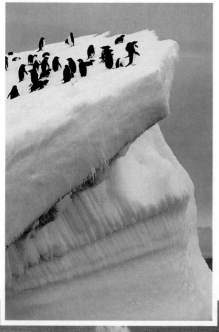

Figure 3–1 *Most water on Earth is salt water found in the oceans. Only a small percent is fresh water, most of which is trapped as ice in the polar icecaps. That leaves only a small portion of fresh water available for use by living things.*

Fresh water makes up only about 3 percent of the Earth's water. However, most of this fresh water cannot be used because it is frozen, mainly in the icecaps near the North and South poles and in glaciers. In fact, only about 15 percent of the Earth's fresh water can be used by living things. This extremely small percent represents the Earth's total supply of fresh water. With such a limited supply, you might wonder why the Earth does not run out of fresh water. Fortunately, the Earth's supply of fresh water is continuously being renewed.

The Water Cycle

Most of the fresh water on the Earth's surface is found in moving water and in standing water. Rivers, streams, and springs are moving water. Ponds, lakes, and swampy wetlands are standing water.

Water moves among these sources of fresh water, the salty oceans, the air, and the land in a cycle. A cycle has no beginning and no end. It is a continuous chain of events. The **water cycle** is the movement of water from the oceans and freshwater sources to the air and land and finally back to the oceans. The water cycle, also called the hydrologic cycle, constantly renews the Earth's supply of fresh water.

Three main steps make up the water cycle. The first step involves the heat energy given off by the sun. This energy causes water on the surface of the Earth to change to water vapor, the gas phase of water. This process is called **evaporation** (ih-vap-uh-RAY-shuhn). Enormous amounts of water evaporate from the oceans. Water also evaporates from freshwater sources and from the soil. Animals and plants release water vapor into the air as well. You might be surprised to learn just how much water actually evaporates into the air from a single plant. (As you might suspect, a scientist has measured it!) In one day, a single large tree can move more than 1800 liters of water from the ground, through its stems and branches, to its leaves, and finally into the air! Other organisms do not move quite the same amount of water as this single large tree. But if you consider the vast number of plants, animals, and other living things that are part of the water cycle, you can see that the total amount of water given off by living things is very large indeed.

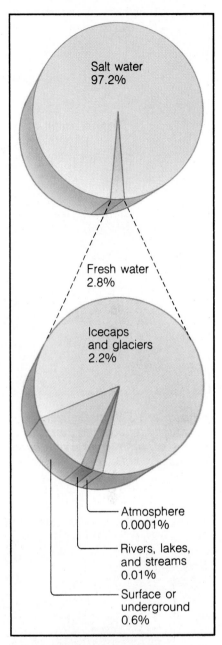

Figure 3–2 *This graph shows the distribution of Earth's water. What percent is fresh water? Is all this water available for use? Explain.*

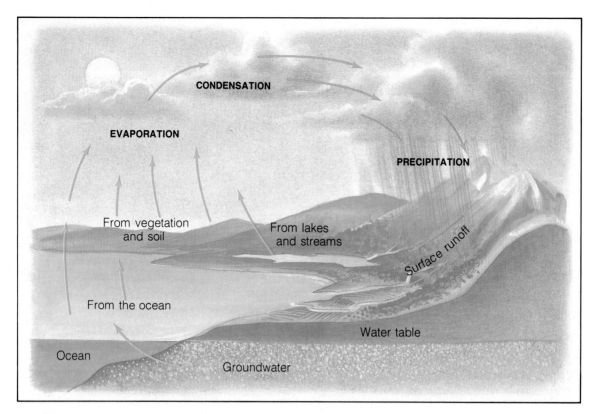

Figure 3–3 *The water cycle constantly renews the Earth's supply of fresh water. What three processes make up the water cycle?*

Figure 3–4 *A large tree can release up to 1800 liters of water a day into the atmosphere. By what process does liquid water in a tree become water vapor in the atmosphere?*

The second step of the water cycle involves a process called **condensation** (kahn-dehn-SAY-shuhn). Condensation is the process by which water vapor changes back into a liquid. For condensation to occur, the air containing the water vapor must be cooled. And this is exactly what happens as the warm air close to the Earth's surface rises. As it moves farther from the Earth's surface, the warm air cools. Cool air cannot hold as much water vapor as warm air. In the cooler air, most of the water vapor condenses into droplets of water that form clouds. But these clouds are not "salty" clouds. Do you know why? When water evaporates from the oceans, the salt is left behind. Water vapor is made of fresh water only.

During the third step of the cycle, water returns to the Earth in the form of rain, snow, sleet, or hail. This process is called **precipitation** (prih-sihp-uh-TAY-shuhn). Precipitation occurs when the water droplets that form in clouds become too numerous and too heavy to remain afloat in the air. The water that falls as rain, snow, sleet, or hail is fresh water. After the water falls, some of it returns to the

Figure 3–5 *The third step of the water cycle is precipitation, which may occur as rain, snow, sleet, or hail.*

atmosphere through evaporation. The cycle of water movement continues. The Earth's supply of fresh water is continuously renewed.

Some of the water that falls as precipitation may run off into ponds, lakes, streams, rivers, or oceans. Some may soak into the ground and become **groundwater.** Groundwater is the water that remains in the ground. At some point, the groundwater flows underground to the oceans. You will learn more about groundwater in the next section.

Frozen Water

If you make a snowball out of freshly fallen snow and hold it tightly in your hands for awhile, the warmth of your body will cause the snow to melt. Snow is actually a solid form of water. You may also notice that some of the snow pressed together by your hands forms ice. The same thing happens when new snow falls on top of old snow. The pressure of the piled-up snow causes some of the snow to change into ice. In time, a **glacier** forms. A glacier is a huge mass of moving ice and snow.

ACTIVITY

DISCOVERING

Making a Model of the Water Cycle

1. Stir salt into a small jar filled with water until no more will dissolve. Pour a 1-cm deep layer of the salt water into a large, wide-mouthed jar.

2. Place a paper cup half filled with sand in the center of the jar.

3. Loosely cover the jar's mouth with plastic wrap. Seal the wrap around the jar's sides with a rubber band.

4. Place a small rock or weight on the plastic wrap directly over the paper cup.

5. Place the jar in direct sunlight. After several hours, observe the setup. Carefully remove the plastic wrap and try to collect a few drops of the water that cling to the undersurface. Taste this water.

What is the purpose of sealing the jar? What did you notice about the taste of the water? What processes of the water cycle are in this model?

■ Develop another model to show the effect of temperature on the water cycle.

The Water Cycle

Write a 250-word essay describing the water cycle. Use the following words in your essay:

water cycle
vapor
evaporation
condensation
precipitation
groundwater
surface runoff
watershed

Glaciers form in very cold areas, such as high in mountains and near the North and the South poles. Because of the extremely cold temperatures in these areas, the snow that falls does not melt completely. As more snow falls, it covers the older snow. As the snow builds up, the pressure on the older snow squeezes the snow crystals together. Eventually ice forms. When the layers of ice become very thick and heavy, the ice begins to move.

Glaciers contain about 2 percent of the available fresh water on the Earth. As sources of fresh water become more scarce, scientists are trying to develop ways to use this frozen supply of fresh water.

VALLEY GLACIERS   Long, narrow glaciers that move downhill between the steep sides of mountain valleys are called **valley glaciers.** Usually, valley glaciers follow channels formed in the past by running water. As a valley glacier moves downhill, it bends and twists to fit the shape of the surrounding land. The valley walls and the weight of the ice itself keep the glacier from breaking apart. But on its surface, the ice cracks. Cracks on the surface of glaciers are called crevasses (krih-VAS-sehz).

As a valley glacier slides downward, it tears rock fragments from the mountainside. The rock fragments become frozen in the glacier. They cut deep grooves in the valley walls. Finer bits of rock smooth the surfaces of the valley walls in much the same way

Figure 3–6 *Valley glaciers are long, narrow glaciers that move downhill between mountain valleys. Here you see valley glaciers in the Alps (left) and in Alaska (right).*

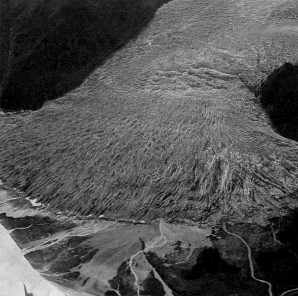

Figure 3-7 *A crevasse, or crack in a glacier, can make mountain climbing a difficult sport indeed.*

as a carpenter's sandpaper smooths the surface of a piece of wooden furniture.

Mountains located anywhere from the equator to the poles can contain glaciers. Many glaciers are found in the United States. Mount Rainier in Washington State and Mount Washington in New Hampshire contain small glaciers. Glaciers can also be found in many mountains of Alaska.

As a valley glacier moves, some of the ice begins to melt, forming a stream of water. This water is called meltwater. Meltwater is usually nearly pure water. Some cities use meltwater as a source of their drinking water. Boulder, Colorado, uses meltwater from the nearby Arapaho Glacier. Meltwater is also used in some places to generate electricity in hydroelectric plants. But some problems arise in the use of meltwater in these ways. Building channels or pipelines to transport meltwater from glaciers to cities can be costly. And the construction of hydroelectric plants in the underdeveloped areas where glaciers are located could alter the surrounding environment.

CONTINENTAL GLACIERS In the polar regions, snow and ice have built up to form thick sheets. These thick sheets of ice are called **continental glaciers,** or polar ice sheets. Continental glaciers cover millions of square kilometers of the Earth's surface and may be several thousand meters thick. Continental glaciers move slowly in all directions.

Figure 3-8 *Continental glaciers such as Mertz Glacier in Antarctica cover millions of square kilometers.*

Continental glaciers are found in Greenland and Antarctica. Nearly 85 percent of Greenland is covered by ice. More than 98 percent of Antarctica is covered by ice. These huge glaciers are more than 4800 meters thick at the center. In the future, continental glaciers could be another source of fresh water.

ICEBERGS At the edge of the sea, continental glaciers form overhanging cliffs. Large chunks of ice, called **icebergs,** often break off from these cliffs and drift into the sea. Some icebergs are as large as the state of Rhode Island! The continental glaciers of Greenland and Antarctica are the major sources of icebergs in ocean waters.

Icebergs can pose a major hazard to ships. In 1912, the ocean liner *Titanic* sank after smashing into an iceberg in the North Atlantic Ocean. Many lives were lost as this ship, thought to be unsinkable, plunged to the ocean bottom on her first voyage. Today, sea lanes are patrolled constantly by ships and planes on the lookout for icebergs.

Much fresh water is frozen in icebergs. Attempts have been made to develop ways of towing icebergs to areas that need supplies of fresh water, such as deserts. But transporting icebergs from Greenland and Antarctica poses several problems. First, the effects of an iceberg on local weather conditions must be evaluated. Second, the cost and time involved in moving the iceberg must be considered.

Figure 3-9 *Icebergs, which often have spectacular shapes, are large chunks of ice that break off glaciers and drift into the sea. Only a small part of an iceberg rises above the water's surface. Can you explain the meaning of the phrase "tip of the iceberg"?*

Third, scientists would have to find a way of preventing the iceberg from melting during the ocean journey. Can you think of ways to use icebergs?

Running Water

Rivers and streams are important sources of fresh water. Many cities and towns were built near rivers and streams. The water is used for irrigating crops, generating electricity, drinking, and other household uses. Rivers and streams are also used for recreational purposes, such as fishing, swimming, and boating. Industry and commerce depend on rivers for transporting supplies and equipment and for shipping finished products. River and stream water is also used to cool certain industrial processes. In the past, industries and towns used rivers and streams as natural sewers to carry away waste products. Today, although pollution is still a problem, strict controls regulate the kinds and amounts of wastes that can be dumped into rivers and streams.

Rain and melted snow that do not evaporate or soak into the soil flow into rivers and streams. The water that enters a river or stream after a heavy rain or during a spring thaw of snow or ice is called **surface runoff.**

The amount of surface runoff is affected by several factors. One factor is the type of soil the precipitation falls on. Some soils soak up more water

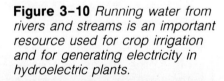
Figure 3–10 *Running water from rivers and streams is an important resource used for crop irrigation and for generating electricity in hydroelectric plants.*

Figure 3–11 *Over the course of millions of years, the Colorado River has carved the Grand Canyon out of the Earth's rocky crust.*

than others. These soils have more spaces between their particles. The space between particles of soil is called **pore space.** The more pore space a soil has, the more water it will hold. The condition of the soil also affects the amount of runoff. If the soil is dry, it will soak up a great deal of water and reduce the surface runoff. If the soil is wet, it will not soak up much water. Surface runoff will increase.

The number of plants growing in an area also affects the amount of surface runoff. Plant roots absorb water from the soil. In areas where there are many plants, large amounts of water are absorbed. There is less surface runoff. The season of the year is another factor that affects the amount of surface runoff. There will be more runoff during rainy seasons and during the spring in areas where large amounts of snow are melting.

A land area in which surface runoff drains into a river or a system of rivers and streams is called a **watershed.** Watersheds vary in size. Especially large watersheds can cover millions of acres and drain their water into the oceans. Watersheds prevent floods and water shortages by controlling the amount of water that flows into streams and rivers. Watersheds also help to provide a steady flow of fresh water into the oceans. How do you think the construction of roads in a watershed area might affect nearby rivers and streams?

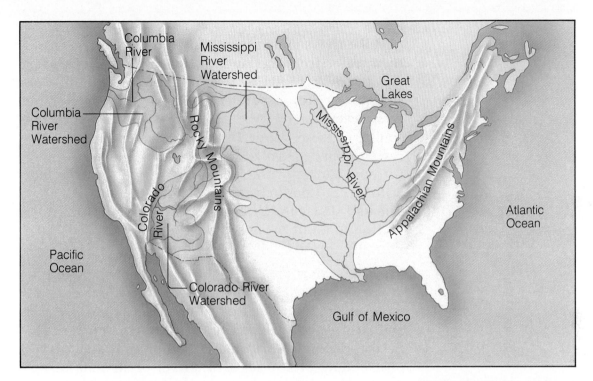

Many rivers are sources of fresh water. The amount of water in a river and the speed at which the water flows affect the usefulness of a river as a source of fresh water. Rivers that move quickly carry a lot of water. But because the water is moving rapidly, fast-moving rivers also carry a large amount of soil, pebbles, and other sediments. The water in these rivers often looks cloudy. Slow-moving rivers do not churn up as much sediment. Their water is clearer. These rivers are better sources of fresh water.

In recent years, pollution has had an effect on the usefulness of rivers and streams as sources of fresh water. If a river or stream has many factories along its banks that discharge wastes into the water, the water becomes polluted. Water in a polluted river or stream must be cleaned before it can be used. Some rivers are so heavily polluted that they cannot be used as a source of fresh water.

Standing Water

Within a watershed, some of the surface runoff gets caught in low places. Standing bodies of fresh water are formed there. Depending on their size, these standing bodies of water are called lakes or ponds.

Figure 3–12 *The major watersheds of the United States are shown in this map. Which watershed is the largest?*

Figure 3–13 *Our supply of fresh water is reduced every year by dangerous wastes released into the water. In what ways can you personally reduce water pollution?*

Activity Bank

How Does a Fish Move?, p.168

Like rivers and streams, lakes and ponds receive their water from the land. Surface runoff keeps lakes and ponds from drying up. In many areas, these standing bodies of water are important sources of fresh water. Moosehead Lake, in Maine, is a natural source of fresh water. It is 56 kilometers long and varies from 3 to 16 kilometers wide. The pine-forested shores of the lake hold huge amounts of water from rains and melting snow. The water is released slowly to the lake, so flooding is not likely. During times of drought (long periods with little rainfall), the lake holds water in reserve.

LAKES AND PONDS Lakes are usually large, deep depressions in the Earth's crust that have filled with fresh water. Rain, melting snow, water from springs and rivers, and surface runoffs fill these depressions. A lake is sometimes formed when there is a natural obstruction, or blockage, of a river or stream. Lakes can be found in many places on the Earth. They are found most frequently at relatively high altitudes and in areas where glaciers were once present.

Ponds are shallow depressions in the Earth's crust that have filled with fresh water. They are usually smaller and not as deep as lakes. Because the water is shallow, sunlight can penetrate to the bottom of a pond. Plants need light to make food, so plants can be found throughout a pond. Lakes, however, often have very deep parts where sunlight cannot reach. Will you find plants at the bottom of a deep lake?

Figure 3–14 *Standing water is found in lakes and ponds throughout the world. What is the difference between a lake and a pond?*

RESERVOIRS The most frequently used sources of fresh water are artificial lakes known as **reservoirs** (REHZ-uhr-vwahrz). A reservoir is built by damming a stream or river that runs through a low-lying area. When the stream or river is dammed, water backs up behind the dam, forming a reservoir. Reservoirs have been built near cities and towns and in mountainous regions throughout the country.

Reservoirs serve several purposes. They help to prevent flooding by controlling water during periods of heavy rain and runoff. Reservoirs store water. During periods when rainfall and runoff are scarce, reservoirs serve as sources of drinking water for nearby towns and cities. In certain areas, reservoirs provide irrigation water for farms. The water held in reservoirs can also be used to generate electricity. Hydroelectric generators are built in the walls of a dam. The water stored in the reservoir can generate electricity when it moves through turbines, which are connected to the dams. Hydroelectric plants convert the energy of moving water into electrical power.

A reservoir, however, cannot be used for all purposes at the same time. Why is this so? Suppose a reservoir is used to store water. To use the water to generate electricity, the water would have to be drawn from the reservoir. The reservoir would no longer be storing water.

Figure 3–15 *The effects of a drought in California in 1991 can be seen in the low water level in the San Luis Reservoir.*

3–1 Section Review

1. What are the major sources of fresh water on the Earth's surface?
2. How much of the Earth's supply of fresh water is available for use? Where is the bulk of fresh water on Earth found?
3. Briefly outline the water cycle.

Critical Thinking—*Applying Concepts*
4. A builder wants to level all the trees in a watershed area to construct homes. What would be some effects of the builder's actions on the watershed and on nearby rivers and streams?

ACTIVITY

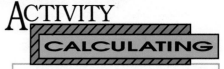

Hydroelectric Power

The total potential hydroelectric power of the world is 2.25 billion kilowatts. Only 363 million kilowatts of this is actually being utilized, however. The United States uses one sixth of the world's hydroelectric power. Calculate the percent of the world's hydroelectric power that is actually being used. What percent of the world's hydroelectric power is used in the United States?

CONNECTIONS

Water, Water Everywhere—And Everyone Wants to Use It

There is nothing more soothing than the sound of raindrops hitting a windowpane. Most outdoor activities are postponed during a heavy rain. But you can be sure that the rain will eventually stop, and the sun will shine once again. You might not be happy when it rains, but you should be thankful. For rain replenishes the Earth's supply of fresh water.

People make great demands on the Earth's supply of fresh water. The average American family uses 760 liters of water a day—and not just to satisfy their thirsts. About half of that total is used to flush away wastes and for showers and baths. Seventy-five liters or more is used each time a dishwasher or a clothes washer cleans up after us.

Water is needed by all forms of life on Earth. Without water, Earth would be a dry and lifeless planet. Visit a desert after a heavy rain and you will see plants appear in the once dry, blowing sands. These plants take advantage of the rain to flower and make seeds before the soil again becomes too dry to support life.

The *technology* to manufacture the many products that contribute to our way of life takes water—often a great deal of water. For example, about 3.8 million liters of water are used to produce a ton of copper—the metal used to make electric wires and the pennies jingling in your pocket. Almost 1.1 million liters of water are used to make a ton of aluminum—a metal used to make cooking utensils and food containers. It even takes about 3.7 liters of water to make a single page in this textbook. We hope you feel that this was water well used!

3-2 Fresh Water Beneath the Surface of the Earth

Not all of the water that falls to the Earth as rain, snow, sleet, or hail runs off into lakes, ponds, rivers, and streams. Some of the water soaks into the ground. Water contained in the ground is one of the Earth's most important natural resources. There is more fresh water below the surface of the land than in all the lakes and reservoirs on the Earth's surface.

Groundwater

If you live in a rural, or country, area, you probably do not get your water from a reservoir or river. More likely, your water is pumped from a well in the ground. As you learned in the previous section, the water stored in the ground is known as groundwater. In many areas, groundwater provides a continuous supply of fresh water.

Groundwater is present because the various forms of precipitation—rain, snow, sleet, and hail—do not stop traveling when they hit the ground. Instead, the precipitation continues to move slowly downward through pores, or spaces, in the rocks and soil. If the rocks and soil have many pores between their particles, they can hold large quantities of groundwater. Sand and gravel are two types of soil that contain many pores.

As the water seeps down, it passes through layers of rocks and soil that allow it to move quickly. Material through which water can move quickly is described as **permeable** (PER-mee-uh-buhl). Sandstone is a rock that is very permeable. But clay, which has small pores between its particles, is not as permeable. Clay is sometimes described as **impermeable.**

UNDERGROUND ZONES Groundwater continues to move downward through permeable rock and soil until it reaches an impermeable layer of rock. When it reaches an impermeable layer, it can go no farther. So the groundwater begins to fill up all the pores above the impermeable layer. This underground region in which all the pores are

Figure 3-16 *Some of the water that falls to Earth as rain, snow, sleet, or hail soaks into the ground. In some places this water is very close to the Earth's surface. So a well such as this can be used to obtain water.*

filled with water is called the **zone of saturation** (sach-uh-RAY-shuhn).

An example from the kitchen may help you to understand what happens when spaces in the ground become filled with water. You may never have looked closely at the sponge on a kitchen sink. When a sponge is barely moist, only some of the spaces in the sponge are filled with water. Most of the spaces hold air. When you place the sponge in water, it swells. Eventually, all the spaces are filled and the sponge cannot take up any more water. The ground acts in much the same way as the sponge. Once the spaces in the ground are filled, the ground is saturated. It cannot hold any more water.

Above the water-filled zone, the ground is not as wet. Pores in the soil and rocks are filled mostly with air. This drier region in which the pores are filled mostly with air is called the **zone of aeration.**

The surface between the zone of saturation and the zone of aeration is an important boundary. It

Figure 3–17 *A cross section of the zones of underground water is shown here. What separates the zone of aeration from the zone of saturation?*

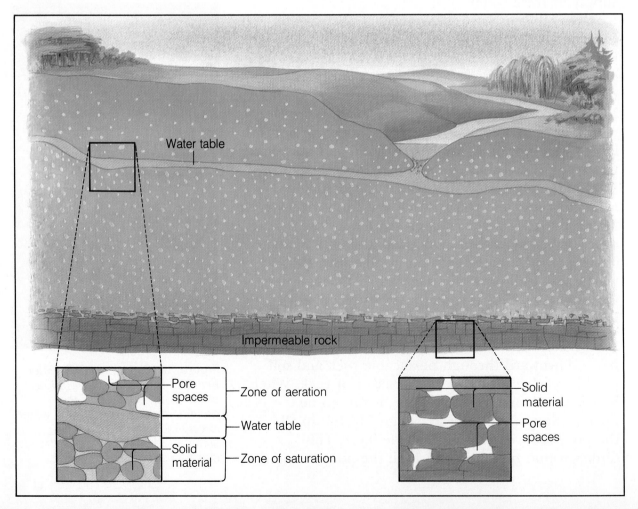

Water table

Impermeable rock

Pore spaces

Solid material

Zone of aeration

Water table

Zone of saturation

Solid material

Pore spaces

Figure 3–18 *What factors influence the levels of the water table in this marsh (left) and at this Saharan oasis (right)?*

marks the level below which the ground is saturated, or soaked, with water. This level is called the **water table.** See Figure 3–17.

At the seashore, the water table is easy to find. After you dig down 10 or 20 centimeters, you may notice that the hole you are digging fills with water. At this point, you have located the water table. In general, the water table is not very deep near a large body of water.

In areas near hills or mountains, the water table may be deep within the ground. In low-lying areas such as valleys with swamps and marshes, the water table may be close to or at the surface. The depth of the water table also varies with the climate of an area. It may be deep in very dry areas, such as deserts. It may be close to the surface in wet, low-lying forest areas. In very moist climate regions, the water table may come right to the surface and form a swamp, lake, or spring. Why do you think low-lying areas have a water table that is close to the surface?

Even in the same area, the depth of the water table may change. Heavy rains and melting snows will make the water table rise. If there is a long, dry period, the water table will fall. The depth of the water table will also change if wells are overused or if many wells are located in a small area. Wells are

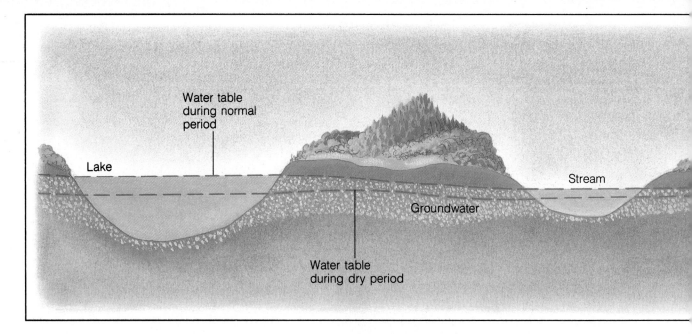

Figure 3-19 *The water table follows the shape of the land. Springs, swamps, and ponds sometimes form where the water table meets the land's surface. What happens to the water table during a dry period?*

holes drilled or dug to the water table to bring water to the surface. The use of several wells in an area may draw so much water from the water table that only very deep wells are able to pump water to the surface. Figure 3-19 shows some characteristics of the water table.

The depth of the water table may have other effects. In order to provide a proper foundation for a tall building, a builder must dig a deep hole. In some places in New York City, the water table is very high, and water rapidly fills the foundation hole. This water must be pumped out in order for construction to proceed. This extra work adds to the cost of a building. In certain areas, wells are dug to provide a source of household water. It is relatively inexpensive to dig a well in areas where the water table is high. In areas where the water table is deep, however, it can be very expensive to dig a well. Remember—a water table is always present, no matter where you live. And you will always reach it if you dig deep enough!

AQUIFERS As groundwater moves through a permeable rock layer, it often reaches an impermeable rock layer or the water table. At this point, the groundwater may move sideways through a layer of rock or sediment that allows it to pass freely. Such a layer is called an **aquifer** (AK-wuh-fer). Aquifers are

Spring

Stream

Swamp

Sea

usually layers of sandstone, gravel, sand, or cracked limestone.

Because rocks form in layers, a layer of permeable rock may become trapped between two layers of impermeable rock. Sandstone (permeable rock) trapped between two layers of shale (impermeable rock) is an example. If the layer of sandstone contains water, an aquifer forms. An aquifer may also form when soil saturated with groundwater is located above an impermeable rock layer.

An aquifer is a source of groundwater. To reach this water, a well is often dug or drilled into the aquifer. Groundwater moves into the well hole and forms a pool. Each time water is pumped from the well, more water moves through the aquifer into the well hole. Nassau and Suffolk counties in New York State pump much of the water used by their inhabitants from huge aquifers.

Because water often moves great distances through aquifers, these underground water sources are extremely vulnerable to pollution. Any pollutants added to an aquifer may spread through the aquifer, endangering water sources far from the pollutants' point of origin.

In some places where the underground rock layers slope, an aquifer carries water from a higher altitude to a lower altitude. If the aquifer is trapped between two layers of impermeable rock, pressure may build up at the lower altitude. A well

ACTIVITY

DISCOVERING

Drought and the Water Table

1. Fill a deep clear-glass baking dish about halfway with sand. Make sure that the sand covers the bottom.

2. Slowly add enough water so that 1 cm of water is visible above the surface of the sand.

3. Add more sand above the water in only one half of the baking dish.

4. Observe the water level during the next few days.

What changes do you notice in the water level?

■ What different conditions of the water table does your model represent?

■ Design an experiment to show the effect of drought on the water table in an area with a clay soil.

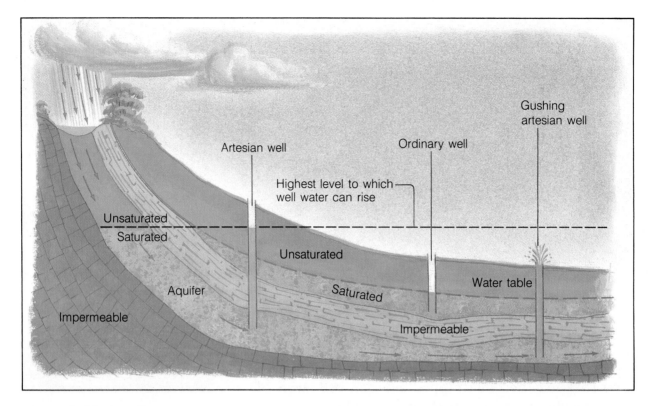

Figure 3–20 *Groundwater can be obtained from an aquifer by means of an ordinary well or an artesian well. The amount of water pressure in an artesian well depends on how close the well is to the water table.*

drilled into the aquifer at this point will provide water without pumping. A well from which water flows on its own without pumping is called an artesian (ahr-TEE-zhuhn) well. See Figure 3–20.

Groundwater Formations

In some areas, the underlying rock is limestone. Because limestone is affected by groundwater in a particular way, underground **caverns** (KAV-ernz) often form in these areas. As water moves down through the soil, it combines with carbon dioxide to form a weak acid that can dissolve limestone. This acid, called carbonic acid, is the weak acid found in seltzer water and other carbonated beverages. You are probably familiar with this weak acid as the "fizz" in a carbonated beverage.

When groundwater enters cracks in limestone, the carbonic acid it contains causes the cracks to become wider. If this process continues long enough, underground passages large enough to walk through may be formed.

Sometimes large underground caverns with many passages are formed. If you walk through these caverns, you will see what looks like long stone icicles

Figure 3–21 *This giant sinkhole in Winter Park, Florida, was caused when groundwater dissolved the limestone base on which part of the town was constructed.*

hanging from the ceilings. These icicles are called stalactites (stuh-LAK-tights). Stalagmites (stuh-LAG-mights) look like stone icicles built up from the floors of the caverns. Stalactites and stalagmites are formed when dissolved substances in groundwater are deposited. You will learn more about the dissolving properties of water in the next section.

Figure 3–22 *In many caverns, underground lakes are formed as groundwater moves through limestone. This lake is found in Hams Caves, Spain. What are the cavern formations hanging from the ceiling and rising from the ground called?*

3–2 Section Review

1. How does groundwater form?
2. What are the three underground zones through which groundwater moves?
3. What causes differences in the depth of the water table?
4. Describe the formation of the following: aquifer, artesian well, cavern.

Connection—*Ecology*
5. Because it is too expensive to truck dangerous pollutants away from the plant, the factory manager proposes that a hole be dug deep in the ground on the side of the factory building and that wastes be dumped into this hole. Predict the effects of this action on the water pumped from wells a short distance from this factory.

3–3 Water as a Solvent

Water is the most common substance on Earth. It exists as a solid, a liquid, or a gas. Water moves in a cycle among the oceans, the air, and the land. Water changes form as it moves through this cycle. In this section, you will take a look at the chemical makeup of water and some of its important properties.

Composition of Water

A water molecule (MAHL-uh-kyool) is the smallest particle of water that has all the properties of water. A water molecule forms when two atoms of hydrogen and one atom of oxygen combine. (Atoms are the basic building blocks of all materials on Earth.) The chemical formula for water is H_2O. As you can see, this formula describes the number of atoms of hydrogen (2) and oxygen (1) that combine to form a water molecule.

In a water molecule, the atom of oxygen has a slight negative charge ($-$). Each atom of hydrogen has a slight positive charge ($+$). So a molecule of water has oppositely charged ends. See Figure 3–23. These charged ends give a water molecule the property known as **polarity** (poh-LAR-uh-tee). You might be familiar with the property of polarity as it applies to a magnet. A magnet has two poles—a positive pole and a negative pole. Each pole attracts the oppositely charged pole of another magnet.

It is the polarity of water molecules that makes water a **solvent** (SAHL-vuhnt). A solvent is a substance in which another substance dissolves. The dissolving process produces a **solution.** A solution contains two or more substances mixed on the molecular level.

For example, if you pour a small quantity of salt into a container of water, the salt will dissolve in the water. Although you will not be able to see the dissolved salt, you will know that it is there if you taste the water. The water molecules, having oppositely charged ends, attract the charged particles that make up the salt. It is as if the water molecules "pull" the charged particles out of the solid salt, dissolving the salt.

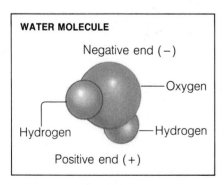

WATER MOLECULE

Negative end ($-$)

Oxygen

Hydrogen — Hydrogen

Positive end ($+$)

Figure 3–23 *A molecule of water exhibits the property of polarity. Why is this property important?*

Because of its polarity, water is able to dissolve many different substances. Water can dissolve so many different substances, in fact, that it is called the universal solvent. You probably use water as a solvent every day without realizing it. For example, flavoring and carbon dioxide gas are dissolved in water to make soft drinks. In fact, all the beverages you drink contain substances dissolved in water. What other products can you name that are made with water?

Farmers use water to dissolve fertilizers for crops. Many medicines use water to dissolve the medication. Certain minerals and chemicals are dissolved in water in water-treatment plants to remove harmful minerals, chemicals, and wastes. For example, chlorine, a chemical that kills bacteria, is added to drinking water. In some cities and towns, fluorides are also added to water. The dissolved fluorides help to prevent tooth decay.

Figure 3–24 In this sewage-treatment plant in California, water hyacinths are used to help purify "dirty" water.

PROBLEM Solving

How Sweet It Is

Several factors affect the rate at which a substance dissolves in water.

Making inferences Use the photographs to determine these factors.

Figure 3–25 *As water evaporates from the hot springs, piles of salts are left behind. Is the water most likely hard or soft? Why?*

ACTIVITY

DISCOVERING

Water as a Solvent

1. Chalk is composed of calcium carbonate, a substance found in many rocks. Add a piece of chalk to a glass of water. To another glass of water, add some quartz sand.

2. Allow both to soak for 30 minutes and then feel each sample.

What happened to the chalk? What happened to the sand? Why do you think certain substances dissolve in water more quickly than others? Why is most beach sand made of quartz?

■ Plan investigations to determine the ability of water to dissolve other substances.

Hardness of Water

The taste, odor, and appearance of water vary from area to area. The differences depend on the amounts and types of materials dissolved in the water.

The water that you drink may come from a surface source or from a groundwater source. This water may be "hard" or "soft." The hardness or softness of water depends on the source of the water and the types of rocks and soils the water comes in contact with. **Hard water** contains large amounts of dissolved minerals, especially calcium and magnesium. Soap will not lather easily in hard water. Also, hard water causes deposits of minerals to build up in water heaters and plumbing systems. **Soft water** does not contain these minerals. Soap lathers easily in soft water, and mineral deposits do not build up when soft water is used.

Some water is softened naturally as it passes through and reacts with rock formations that contain certain minerals. These minerals remove the calcium and magnesium from the water, making it soft. Many homes with hard water have water softeners that remove the minerals that make the water hard. Do you know what type of water you have in your home? How could you experiment to find out?

Quality of Water

Water is necessary to all life on Earth. So it is important to maintain the quality of our water.

Unfortunately, many of Earth's freshwater sources are becoming polluted. In nature, water is usually filtered as it passes through soil and sand. This filtering removes impurities. But the careless dumping of sewage, silt, industrial wastes, and pesticides into water has produced many serious problems. Because so many different substances can be dissolved in water, water is becoming more and more polluted.

Water pollution limits the amount and kinds of wildlife that can live in water. Water pollution also affects supplies of drinking water and destroys recreational areas. Among the chemicals that cause water pollution are nitrates and phosphates. These chemicals are used on farms to improve the growth of plants or to kill harmful insects. Nitrates and phosphates have entered the groundwater in many areas and must be removed before water can be used for drinking or swimming.

Federal laws have been passed to prevent industries from dumping certain chemical wastes into the Earth's waters. Waste-water treatment systems are being built to remove pollution from water before it enters rivers and lakes. Although Earth is called the water planet (and the supply of water seems unending), the truth is that we have a limited supply of fresh water. This water must be protected from sources of pollution. Can you think of some other steps that might be taken to do just this?

Figure 3–26 *One of the most serious problems facing society is the pollution of its water supply. Here you see an oil spill in Galveston Bay, Texas.*

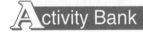

Activity Bank

What Is the Effect of Phosphates on Plant Growth?, p.169

3–3 Section Review

1. Describe the structure of a molecule of water. How is this structure related to its ability to act as a solvent?
2. What is hard water? Soft water?
3. What are three sources of water pollution? Why must the water supply be protected from pollutants?

Critical Thinking—*Designing an Experiment*

4. Design an experiment to compare the hardness of two sources of water using only common, everyday substances. You can use tap water from your home, bottled water, or water from your school or the home of a friend or relative.

Laboratory Investigation

Porosity of Various Soils

Problem

How can the water-holding capability, or porosity, of various soils be determined?

Materials *(per group)*

250 mL sand
250 mL clay
250 mL gravel
4 small paper cups
2 L water
500-mL graduated cylinder

Procedure 🔺

1. Fill the first paper cup about three-fourths full of sand. Fill the second paper cup about three-fourths full of clay. Fill the third paper cup about three-fourths full of gravel. Fill the fourth paper cup about three-fourths full of a mixture of sand, clay, and gravel.

2. Fill the graduated cylinder with water to the 500 mL mark. Slowly pour water into the first cup. Let the water seep through the sand. Slowly add more water until a small pool of water is visible on the surface of the sand. At this point, the sand can hold no more water.

3. Determine the amount of water you added to the sand by subtracting the amount of water left in the graduated cylinder from 500 mL. Record this figure in the appropriate place in a data table similar to the one shown here.

4. Repeat steps 2 and 3 for the cups of clay, gravel, and the mixture of sand, clay, and gravel.

Observations

1. Which soil sample holds the most water?
2. Which soil sample holds the least water?

Soil	Amount of Water Added to Soil
Sand	
Clay	
Gravel	
Sand, clay, gravel	

Analysis and Conclusions

1. Why can some soil samples hold more water than others?
2. What can you conclude about the porosity of the soil samples you used?
3. If you wished to test the porosity of the soil found on your school grounds, what procedure would you follow? Which tested soil sample do you think the soil of the grounds at your school would most resemble?
4. **On Your Own** What effects, if any, do the roots of plants have on the porosity of soil? Design an experiment to test your hypothesis.

Study Guide

Summarizing Key Concepts

3–1 Fresh Water on the Surface of the Earth

▲ Fresh water—one of the Earth's most precious resources—is found in lakes, ponds, rivers, streams, springs, and glaciers.

▲ The water cycle is the continuous movement of water from the oceans and sources of fresh water to the air and land and then back to the oceans.

▲ The three steps in the water cycle are evaporation, condensation, and precipitation.

▲ A land area in which surface runoff drains into a river or system of streams and rivers is called a watershed.

3–2 Fresh Water Beneath the Surface of the Earth

▲ Fresh water beneath the ground's surface is called groundwater.

▲ The water table is the underground level below which all the pore spaces are filled with water. The water table separates the zone of aeration from the zone of saturation.

▲ The depth of the water table depends on the location of groundwater, the climate of the area, the amount of rainfall, the type of soil, and the number of wells drawing water.

▲ Groundwater formations include caverns, stalactites, and stalagmites.

3–3 Water as a Solvent

▲ A molecule of water is made up of two atoms of hydrogen combined with one atom of oxygen.

▲ Because of the polarity of water molecules, water is a good solvent. It can dissolve many substances.

▲ Water may be hard or soft depending on the kinds and amounts of minerals in it.

▲ People must protect and conserve their sources of fresh water.

Reviewing Key Terms

Define each term in a complete sentence.

3–1 Fresh Water on the Surface of the Earth
water cycle
evaporation
condensation
precipitation
groundwater
glacier
valley glacier
continental glacier
iceberg
surface runoff
pore space
watershed
reservoir

3–2 Fresh Water Beneath the Surface of the Earth
permeable
impermeable
zone of saturation
zone of aeration
water table
aquifer
cavern

3–3 Water as a Solvent
polarity
solvent
solution
hard water
soft water

I ■ 105

Chapter Review

Content Review

Multiple Choice

Choose the letter of the answer that best completes each statement.

1. The continuous movement of water from the oceans and freshwater sources to the air and land and back to the oceans is called the
   a. nitrogen cycle.   c. runoff.
   b. water cycle.   d. oxygen cycle.

2. The process in which water vapor changes to a liquid is called
   a. precipitation.   c. condensation.
   b. evaporation.   d. runoff.

3. Very thick sheets of ice found mainly in polar regions are called
   a. aquifers.
   b. crevasses.
   c. valley glaciers.
   d. continental glaciers.

4. The space between soil particles is called
   a. pore space.
   b. zone of aeration.
   c. surface runoff.
   d. polarity.

5. The underground region where all the pores are filled with water is called the
   a. zone of saturation.
   b. aquifer.
   c. watershed.
   d. zone of aeration.

6. The level below which all of the pore spaces in the soil are filled with water is called the
   a. water table.   c. meltwater.
   b. groundwater.   d. watershed.

7. The property of water that enables it to dissolve many substances easily is called
   a. hardness.   c. softness.
   b. polarity.   d. permeability.

8. A substance in which another substance dissolves is called a
   a. solution.
   b. saturated substance.
   c. solvent.
   d. molecule.

True or False

If the statement is true, write "true." If it is false, change the underlined word or words to make the statement true.

1. The process by which water changes to a gas is <u>condensation</u>.
2. Rain, snow, sleet, and hail are all forms of <u>precipitation</u>.
3. Water that enters a river or a stream after a heavy rain or during thawing of snow or ice is called <u>groundwater</u>.
4. In dry desert areas, the water table is usually very <u>shallow</u>.
5. Materials through which water can move quickly are described as <u>saturated</u>.

Concept Mapping

Complete the following concept map for Section 3–1. Refer to pages 16–17 to construct a concept map for the entire chapter.

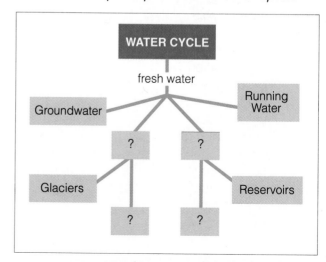

Concept Mastery

Discuss each of the following in a brief paragraph.

1. What is the water cycle? How does this cycle renew the Earth's supply of fresh water?
2. Describe the structure of a molecule of water. How does this structure affect its ability to dissolve substances?
3. What is a watershed? Why are watersheds important?
4. Why is it important to keep from polluting underground sources of water?
5. What is the difference between a lake and a reservoir? How could both bodies of water be used to supply a city with water?
6. Why is it important to protect our sources of fresh water? Why is it important to develop new sources?
7. What is hard water? How does hard water differ from soft water?
8. What is an aquifer? How can aquifers be used as a source of fresh water?

Critical Thinking and Problem Solving

Use the skills you have developed in this chapter to answer each of the following.

1. **Making diagrams** Two different areas of the United States receive the same amount of rainfall during a day. Area A has soil that contains many large pores and rocks made of sandstone. The soil in Area B is mainly heavy clay. Area A is a desert. Area B is a swamp. For each area draw two diagrams: one that shows the level of the water table before a day of rain and one that shows the level after a day of rain.
2. **Designing an experiment** Clouds are not salty. The salt from the oceans is left behind when the water evaporates. Devise an experiment to illustrate this fact. Describe the problem, materials, procedure, expected observations, and your conclusions.

3. **Applying concepts** Water molecules have polarity. Explain how water molecules can attract each other. Illustrate your explanation.
4. **Applying concepts** Pure water evaporates continuously from the oceans while salts are left behind. Explain why the salinity of ocean water does not increase over time.
5. **Relating concepts** A factory dumps harmful chemical wastes into a huge hole dug in the ground behind the building. Explain why and how these chemicals might affect a well located in a town several kilometers away from the factory site.
6. **Designing an experiment** Soap does not lather easily in hard water. It does so, however, in soft water. Devise a simple test to determine if water from a tap in your school is hard or soft.
7. **Using the writing process** Develop an advertising campaign to warn people about the dangers of polluting rivers and streams. You might want to design a poster campaign and/or write a letter to your neighbors to enlist their help.

Earth's Landmasses

Just imagine how hard it would be to visit a strange place for the first time without a map to guide you. Although someone might be able to give you accurate directions to this unfamiliar location, it is certainly easier and more helpful if you look at a map and visualize the trip before you begin.

The same idea holds true for the pilots of an airplane. Without maps, it would be very difficult for an airplane leaving Illinois to arrive in Germany. With accurate maps, however, you can enjoy a frankfurter at a baseball game in Chicago, and the next day eat a knockwurst at a soccer game in Berlin.

Throughout history, as people explored Planet Earth, maps became more and more accurate. By the middle of the eighteenth century, maps showed the Earth's land areas in the same shapes and sizes you see on maps today. Today, map-making is aided by photographs taken by high-flying satellites.

In this chapter, you will learn about different land features. You will also learn how these land features are represented on maps, and you will gain a better understanding of maps in general.

Journal *Activity*

You and Your World If you live in a city or town, make a map of your neighborhood. If you live in a rural area, make a map of the road you live along. Include places of interest and landmarks that would make it easy for a relative or friend to find your home if they wanted to visit you.

◀ *In centuries past, maps of Earth were drawn by the skilled hands of artists. Today a new type of Earth map—made from thousands of images relayed by satellite—shows just how remarkably beautiful Earth is.*

4–1 The Continents

All the land on Earth is surrounded by oceans. There are many **islands**, or small landmasses completely surrounded by water, scattered throughout the oceans. But there are only four major landmasses on Earth. Each major landmass consists of one or more **continents**. A continent is a landmass that measures millions of square kilometers and rises a considerable distance above sea level. Each continent has at least one large area of very old rock exposed at its surface. This area is called a shield. Shields form the cores of the continents. The shield of North America is located in Canada.

There are seven continents on the Earth: Asia, Africa, Europe, Australia, North America, South America, and Antarctica. Some of the continents are joined to form a single landmass. See Figure 4–2. For example, Asia and Europe are joined together as one landmass, called Eurasia. And Africa is connected to Asia by a small piece of land. These three continents—Asia, Africa, and Europe—make up one giant landmass, the largest landmass on Earth.

The second largest landmass consists of the continents of North America and South America. Central America is located just to the south of North America. Central America is part of the North American continent. At the point where Central America connects to South America, the continents of North America and South America are joined.

The third largest landmass is the continent of Antarctica. Antarctica is about twice the size of the United States. Antarctica has only recently been explored. In fact, the first known exploration of Antarctica occurred in 1901.

Antarctica is very different from the other continents. It is almost completely covered by a thick icecap. In fact, the Antarctic icecap is the largest in

Figure 4–1 *Mount Everest is considered to be the highest point on Earth. The lowest point on Earth is the Dead Sea. The difference in altitude between these two points is 9200 meters!*

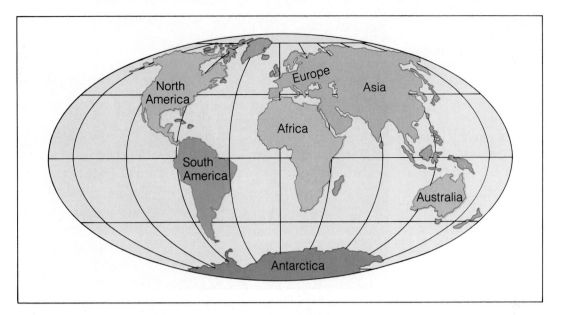

Figure 4-2 *This map shows the major islands and the seven continents of the world. Which continents make up the Earth's largest landmass?*

the world and covers an area of 34 million square kilometers! The Antarctic icecap is so large that it extends into the surrounding ocean. It contains almost 90 percent of the ice on the Earth's surface.

Antarctica is certainly the coldest area on Earth. In July 1983, the temperature in Vostok, Antarctica, dropped to nearly −89.2°C, the lowest temperature ever recorded on Earth. Many scientific stations have been built on Antarctica. Some scientific teams study life on the continent. Others study the land beneath the ice. Still others study conditions in the atmosphere over Antarctica. Today, one of the major areas of study is the depletion of the ozone layer over Antarctica. In the past several years, "holes" in the ozone layer have been observed there. Scientists study these areas in an attempt to determine the long-term effects of ozone depletion. Because of the extreme cold, however, the scientists who live and work in Antarctica are only temporary visitors to this continent.

Australia is the smallest landmass still considered a continent. It is the only continent that is a single country. Sometimes, Australia is referred to as the island continent. Why do you think this term is used to describe Australia?

ACTIVITY

CALCULATING

Comparing the Continents

1. From a globe, trace the outline of each of the seven continents. Cut out the outlines. Trace each outline on a piece of graph paper. Shade in the outlined continents.

2. Consider each square on the graph paper as an area unit of 1. Calculate the area units for each of the seven continents to the nearest whole unit. For example, suppose a continent covers all of 45 units, about one half of 20 units, and about one fourth of 16 units. The total area units this continent covers will be 45 + 10 + 4, or 59.

List the continents from the smallest to the largest.

Figure 4–3 *Australia is a continent country completely surrounded by water. These steep cliffs border on the Indian Ocean.*

4–1 Section Review

1. Identify the seven continents.
2. What is a landmass? A continent? An island?
3. What makes the continent of Antarctica unusual? What makes Australia unusual?

Critical Thinking—*Applying Concepts*
4. Predict what would happen if the average temperature of Antarctica rose to 5°C.

Guide for Reading

Focus on this question as you read.

▶ *What are the three main types of landscape regions?*

4–2 Topography

Over billions of years, the surface of the Earth has changed many times. These changes are produced by several factors. Weather conditions such as wind and heat change the surface. Running water reshapes the land. Earthquakes and volcanoes cause major changes in the Earth's surface. Earthquakes can build up or level mountains, and volcanoes can produce new islands. Surtsey, an island off the coast of Iceland, was produced in 1963 by volcanic eruptions on the seabed. Even people alter the Earth's appearance. For example, they use huge earth-moving machinery to smooth the Earth's surface in order to construct the buildings that make up a large city. What other human activities can you think of that might change the shape of the land?

Scientists refer to the shape of the Earth's surface as its **topography** (tuh-PAHG-ruh-fee). The Earth's topography is made up of different kinds of **landscapes**. A landscape is the physical features of the Earth's surface found in an area. Figure 4–5 shows landscape regions of the United States. In which landscape region do you live?

There are three main types of landscape regions: mountains, plains, and plateaus. Each type has different characteristics. One characteristic of a landscape region is **elevation**, or height above sea level. Some landscape regions have high elevations; others have low elevations. Within a landscape region, the elevation can vary from place to place. The difference in a region's elevations is called its **relief**. If a landscape region has high relief, there are large differences in the elevations of different areas within the landscape region. What do you think is true of a landscape region with low relief?

Figure 4–4 *Earth's landmasses are constantly undergoing changes. The island of Surtsey appeared in 1963 as a result of volcanic eruption on the ocean floor.*

Figure 4–5 *This map shows the major landscape regions of the continental United States. What type of landscape region covers most of the land shown? In what type of landscape region do you live?*

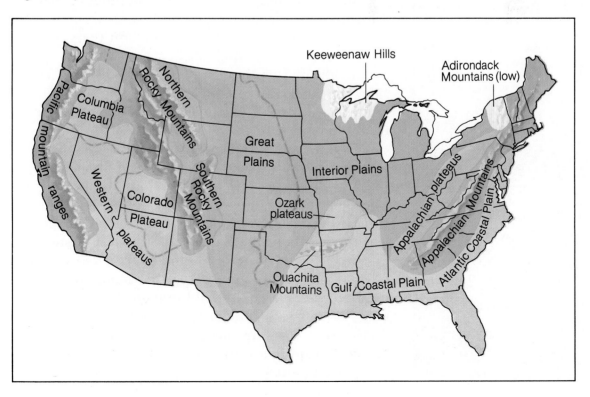

ACTIVITY

CALCULATING

Mountain Landscapes

Mountain landscapes cover about one fifth of the Earth's surface. The total land area of the Earth's surface is about 148,300,000 km². How much of the surface of the Earth has a mountain landscape?

Figure 4–6 *Mountains may form when the Earth's crust breaks into great blocks that are then tilted or lifted (top). Folded mountains form when layers of the Earth's crust wrinkle into wavelike folds (bottom).*

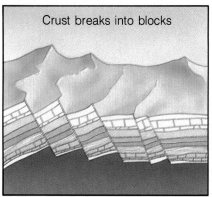

Crust breaks into blocks

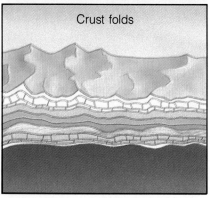

Crust folds

Mountains

Mountains make up one type of landscape region. Mountains are natural landforms that reach high elevations. Mountains have narrow summits, or tops, and steep slopes, or sides. Mountain landscapes have very high relief.

What do you think is the difference between a hill and a mountain? Most geologists agree that a mountainous area rises at least 600 meters above the surrounding land. But the actual height of a mountain is given as its height above sea level. For example, Pike's Peak in Colorado rises about 2700 meters above the surrounding land. But its actual height above sea level is 4301 meters.

The highest mountain in the world is Mount Everest. Mount Everest is part of the Himalayas, a great chain of mountains in Asia that extends from Tibet to Pakistan. The peak of Mount Everest soars more than 8 kilometers! The highest mountain in the United States is Mount McKinley in the state of Alaska. It is more than 6 kilometers high. What mountains are closest to your home?

All mountains did not form at the same time. Some mountains are old; others are relatively young. Mountains are built very slowly. It is thought that the Rocky Mountains began to form about 65 million years ago. It took about 10 million years for these mountains to reach their maximum height. You might be surprised to learn that geologists consider the Rocky Mountains to be "young" mountains. In this case, "young" and "old" are relative terms compared to the age of the Earth.

Mountains can be formed in several ways. Some mountains result from the folding and breaking of the Earth's surface. Other mountains are created when hot magma (liquid rock) from the Earth's interior breaks through the Earth's surface. (You will learn more about the Earth's interior in Chapter 5.)

Streams and rivers in mountain areas move very quickly. The higher and steeper the mountain slopes, the faster the water flows. Mountain streams and rivers carry rocks of all sizes. When there is heavy rainfall or when snow melts, the streams and rivers become so swollen with water that they can even carry small boulders.

Figure 4–7 *Some of the world's mountains are described below. In what state is the highest mountain in North America located?*

SOME OF THE WORLD'S MOST FAMOUS MOUNTAINS

Name	Height Above Sea Level (meters)	Location	Interesting Facts
Aconcagua	6959	Andes in Argentina	Highest mountain in the Western Hemisphere
Cotopaxi	5897	Andes in Ecuador	Highest active volcano in the world
Elbert	4399	Colorado	Highest mountain of Rockies
Everest	8848	Himalayas on Nepal-Tibet border	Highest mountain in the world
K2	8611	Kashmir	Second highest mountain in the world
Kanchenjunga	8598	Himalayas on Nepal-India border	Third highest mountain in the world
Kilimanjaro	5895	Tanzania	Highest mountain in Africa
Logan	5950	Yukon	Highest mountain in Canada
Mauna Kea	4205	On volcanic island in Hawaii	Highest island mountain in the world
Mauna Loa	4169	On volcanic island in Hawaii	Famous volcanic mountain
McKinley	6194	Alaska	Highest mountain in North America
Mitchell	2037	North Carolina	Highest mountain in the Appalachians
Mont Blanc	4807	France	Highest mountain in the Alps
Mount St. Helens	2549	Cascades in Washington	Recent active volcano in the United States
Pikes Peak	4301	Colorado	Most famous of the Rocky Mountains
Rainier	4392	Cascades in Washington	Highest mountain in Washington
Vesuvius	1277	Italy	Only active volcano on the mainland of Europe
Whitney	4418	Sierra Nevadas in California	Highest mountain in California

Figure 4–8 *The Rocky Mountains are considered "young" mountains because they formed a mere 65 million years ago (left). Mountains in the Appalachian Range are "old" mountains, having formed more than 300 million years ago (top right). Mount Kilimanjaro in Africa is an example of a mountain formed by volcanic activity (bottom right).*

Figure 4–9 *This stream, swollen with water from mountain snows, flows quickly.*

Streams and rivers often carve valleys in mountains. Valleys in older mountains are usually wide. Valleys in younger mountains are usually narrow. Why do you think this is so?

Individual mountains, which are mountains that are not part of a group, can be found in all parts of the world. These mountains are usually the products of volcanic activity during which magma broke through the Earth's surface. Examples of volcanic mountains are Fujiyama in Japan, Vesuvius in Italy, and Kilimanjaro in Tanzania.

Most mountains, however, are part of a group of mountains called a **mountain range**. A mountain range is a roughly parallel series of mountains that have the same general shape and structure. A group of mountain ranges in one area is called a **mountain system**. The Great Smoky, Blue Ridge, Cumberland, and Green mountain ranges are all in the Appalachian mountain system in the eastern United States.

Most mountain ranges and mountain systems are part of an even larger group of mountains called a **mountain belt.** The pattern of mountain belts on the Earth is shown in Figure 4–10.

There are two major mountain belts in the world. The Circum-Pacific belt rings the Pacific Ocean. The Eurasian-Melanesian belt runs across northern

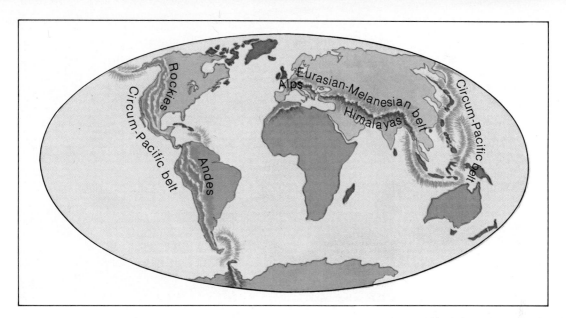

Africa, southern Europe, and Asia. The Eurasian-Melanesian belt and the Circum-Pacific belt meet in Indonesia, just north of Australia. These mountain belts may have been formed by movements of the Earth's crust.

Figure 4–10 *Most of the Earth's mountains are located within the two major mountain belts shown on this map: the Circum-Pacific belt and the Eurasian-Melanesian belt. Which major belt runs through the United States?*

Plains

Another type of landscape region is made up of **plains**. Plains are flat land areas that do not rise far above sea level. Plains, then, have very small differences in elevation. They are areas of low relief. The difference between the highest and lowest elevations in a plain may be less than 100 meters. Plains areas are characterized by broad rivers and streams. Most of the plants that grow well here are grasses, related to the grass plants that are grown in a lawn or on a baseball field. Some plains are located at the edges of a continent. Others are located in the continent's interior.

COASTAL PLAINS A coast is a place where the land meets the ocean. Low, flat areas along the coasts are called **coastal plains.** The Atlantic and Gulf coastal plains of the United States are typical coastal plains. The change in elevation of the land from the Gulf of Mexico to southern Illinois is very small. Over a distance of more than 1000 kilometers, the land rises only about 150 meters above sea level.

The coastal plains of the United States were formed when soil and silt were deposited on the edge of the continent. In the past, shallow oceans

To the Roof of the World

Mount Everest is the highest mountain on Earth. Sir Edmund Hillary was the first person to reach the top of Mount Everest. Hillary described his exploits in a book entitled *High Adventure*. You might enjoy reading *High Adventure* (or any of several other books Hillary wrote describing his various exploits).

Figure 4-11 *This area in Jacksonville Beach, Florida, is located within the Atlantic coastal plain. What characteristic of plains regions is visible in this photograph?*

ctivity Bank

Making Soil, p.171

Figure 4-12 *The land in interior plains regions has fertile soil. In the past, these lands supported huge herds of grazing animals, such as buffaloes. Today crops are grown in these areas.*

covered these areas. As these oceans disappeared, large deposits of sand and silt were left behind. More sediments have been deposited onto coastal plains by rivers and streams. The soil in these areas has been enriched by these deposits.

Because of the abundance of fertile soil, farming is a major activity of great economic importance on coastal plains. In the United States, cotton, tobacco, vegetables, and citrus crops are grown in these areas.

INTERIOR PLAINS Some low flat areas are also found inland on a continent. These areas are called **interior plains**. Interior plains are somewhat higher above sea level than coastal plains. For example, the interior plains of the United States have an elevation of about 450 meters above sea level. This is considerably higher than the elevation of the Atlantic and Gulf coastal plains. But within an interior plain itself, the differences in elevation are small. So interior plains also have low relief.

The Great Plains of the United States are large interior plains. They were formed as mountains and hills that were later worn down by wind, streams, and glaciers. Large interior plains are found in the Soviet Union, central and eastern Europe, and parts of Africa and Australia.

Interior plains have good soil. The sediments deposited by rivers and streams make the soil suitable for farming. In the United States, grasses and grains such as wheat, barley, and oats are grown in the interior plains. Cattle and sheep are raised in these areas, too.

Plateaus

A third type of landscape region consists of **plateaus**. Plateaus are broad, flat areas of land that rise more than 600 meters above sea level. Some plateaus reach elevations of more than 1500 meters. Plateaus are not considered mountains because their surfaces are fairly flat. Like plains, plateaus have low relief. But unlike plains, plateaus rise much higher above sea level.

Most plateaus are located inland. But a few plateaus are near oceans. The plateaus near oceans often end in a cliff at the edge of a coastal plain. If a plateau is directly next to an ocean, it ends in a cliff at the coast.

Plateaus often have the same landscape for thousands of kilometers. Some plateaus have been deeply cut by streams and rivers that form canyons. The Colorado River cuts through the Colorado Plateau to form the Grand Canyon in Arizona. The river flows 1.5 kilometers lower than the surface of the surrounding plateau. Have you ever visited the Grand Canyon or seen pictures of it?

Many plateaus of the world are dry, nearly desert areas. They are often used for grazing cattle, sheep, and goats. Plateaus in the western United States are rich in coal and mineral deposits such as copper and lead.

Figure 4-13 *Plateaus are broad, flat areas of land with low relief. Some plateaus have been cut by streams and rivers that form canyons. Cut by the relentless action of the Colorado River, the Grand Canyon is among the most impressive on Earth.*

Frozen Foods—An Idea From Frigid Lands

Near the North Pole—in climates almost as severe as those found in Antarctica—native peoples have lived for many thousands of years. They survive primarily by fishing and hunting. And a long time ago, they discovered that the extreme cold in which they live can have significant value—it can preserve food.

Clarence Birdseye was a businessman and inventor, who at his death owned more than 300 patents on his inventions. Early in his career, Birdseye traded in furs. In 1912 and 1916 he visited Labrador, a part of Canada. While there, he observed the people freezing food for use in the winter because it was difficult for them to get a fresh supply during the very cold months. Birdseye spent years experimenting on ways to freeze food commercially. In 1929 he achieved success and began selling his quick-frozen foods. As a result of this technology, Birdseye became quite wealthy and famous. Today, his name is practically synonymous with frozen foods.

The idea seems a simple one. Extremely cold temperatures can protect foods from spoiling almost indefinitely. (Some Russian scientists claim that they have eaten the meat of a mammoth frozen 20,000 years ago and have found it edible!) But keep in mind that the original idea came from native peoples whose primary motive was to survive in a cold, hostile environment.

4–2 Section Review

1. What is a landscape? What are the three main landscape types found in the United States?
2. What do scientists mean by the Earth's topography?
3. Describe the following: mountain, mountain range, mountain system, mountain belt.
4. What is a coastal plain? An interior plain?

Connection—*Ecology*

5. Why are plains and plateaus good areas to grow crops, whereas the sides of mountains usually are not?

4–3 Mapping the Earth's Surface

Guide for Reading

Focus on this question as you read.

▶ *What are some features of the Earth shown on maps and globes?*

A **map** is a drawing of the Earth, or a part of the Earth, on a flat surface. There are many ways to show the Earth's surface features on maps. Some maps show only a small area of the Earth. Others show the Earth's entire surface. Maps are often grouped together in a book called an atlas. Have you ever thumbed through an atlas and visited, if only in your imagination, distant and foreign places?

The most accurate representation of the entire surface of the Earth is a **globe**. A globe is a spherical, or round, model of the Earth. It shows the shapes, sizes, and locations of all the Earth's landmasses and bodies of water.

Both maps and globes are drawn to **scale**. A scale compares distances on a map or globe to actual distances on the Earth's surface. For example, 1 centimeter on a map might equal 10 kilometers on the Earth's surface. Different maps may have different scales. However, all maps and globes should have the scale used to represent the distances shown on that particular map or globe. Why is including a scale important?

Meridians

When you look at a globe or a map, you see many straight lines on it. Some of the lines run between the points that represent the geographic North and South poles of the Earth. These lines are called **meridians** (muh-RIHD-ee-uhnz).

Each meridian is half of an imaginary circle around the Earth. Geographers have named the meridian that runs through Greenwich, England, the **prime meridian**. Because meridians run north and south, they measure distance east and west. The

Figure 4–14 *Satellites that orbit the Earth provide information used to make maps. In the center of the photograph of Washington, DC, you can make out the mall that runs from the United States Capitol to the Washington Monument. Satellite images can also show evidence of living organisms. The yellow areas in the photograph represent great numbers of microscopic life in the oceans along the coasts of continents.*

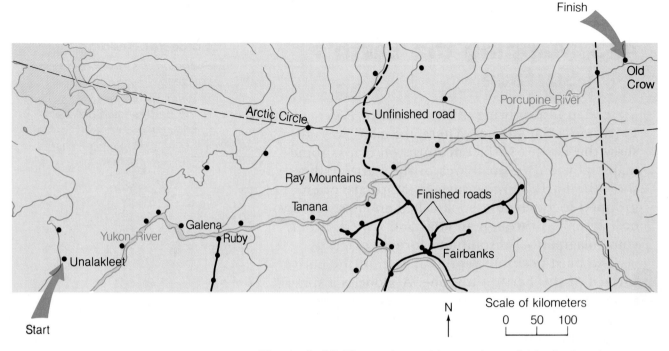

Finish

Old Crow

Porcupine River

Arctic Circle

Unfinished road

Ray Mountains

Finished roads

Tanana

Galena

Ruby

Yukon River

Unalakleet

Fairbanks

N

Scale of kilometers

0   50   100

Start

Figure 4-15 *The scale on this map is useful in finding the distance between two cities. If you took a plane ride from Unalakleet to Old Crow, how many kilometers would you fly?*

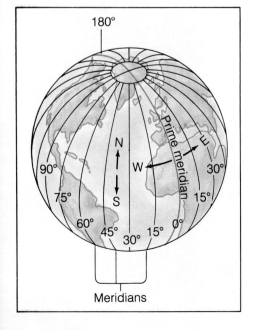

180°

90°

75°

60°

45°

30°

15°

0°

15°

30°

Prime meridian

N

W

S

E

Meridians

measure of distance east and west of the prime meridian is called **longitude**. Meridians are used to measure longitude.

The distance around any circle, including the Earth, is measured in degrees. The symbol for degree is a small circle written at the upper right of a number. All circles contain 360°. Each meridian marks 1° of longitude around the Earth. But not all meridians are drawn on most globes or maps. (Just think how crowded a map would look if all 360 meridians were drawn.)

The prime meridian is labeled 0° longitude. Meridians to the east of the prime meridian are called east longitudes. Meridians to the west of the prime meridian are called west longitudes. Meridians of east longitude measure distances halfway around the Earth from the prime meridian. Meridians of west longitude measure distances around the other half of the Earth from the prime meridian. Because half the distance around a circle is 180°, meridians of east and west longitude go from 0° to 180°.

Figure 4-16 *Meridians are lines running north to south on a map or globe. What are meridians used to measure?*

Time Zones

On Earth, a day is 24 hours long. During these 24 hours, the Earth makes one complete rotation. You can think of this in another way. In one day, the Earth rotates 360°. If you divide 360° by the number of hours in a day (24), you will find that the Earth rotates 15° every hour. Thus the Earth has been divided into 24 zones of 15° of longitude each. These zones are called **time zones**. A time zone is a longitudinal belt of the Earth in which all areas have the same local time.

Suppose it is 6:00 AM in Miami, Florida. It is also 6:00 AM in Washington, DC, because Miami and Washington are in the same time zone. But it is not 6:00 AM in Dallas, Texas. Dallas is one time zone away from Miami and Washington. How can you tell whether it is earlier or later in Texas?

Figure 4–17 *The Earth has been divided into 24 time zones. All areas within a single time zone have the same local time.*

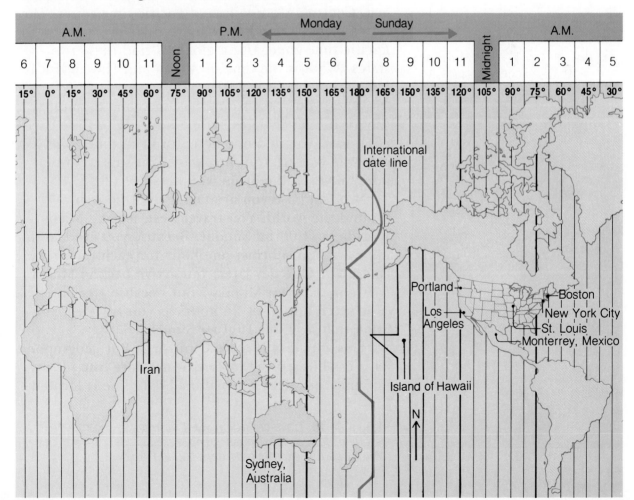

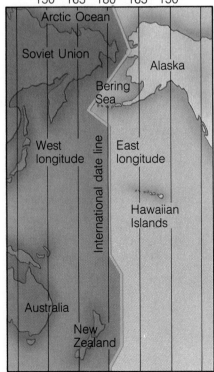

The Earth rotates on its axis from west to east. This direction of rotation makes the sun appear to rise in the east and travel toward the west. So the sun comes into view first in the east. Suppose the sun rises in New York City at 6:00 AM. After the Earth rotates 15°, the sun rises in Dallas. It is 6:00 AM in Dallas. But it is now 7:00 AM in New York City. Dallas is one time zone west of New York City.

After the Earth rotates another 15°, the sun rises in Denver. It is 6:00 AM in Denver. But by now it is 7:00 AM in Dallas and 8:00 AM in New York City. Denver is one time zone west of Dallas and two time zones west of New York City.

If it were not for time zones, the sun would rise in New York City at 6:00 AM, in Dallas at 7:00 AM, in Denver at 8:00 AM, and in Los Angeles at 9:00 AM. And the sun would not rise in Hawaii until 11:00 AM! Because of time zones, the sun rises at 6:00 AM in each city. Is this an advantage? Why?

There are four time zones in the contiguous United States. From east to west they are: the Eastern, Central, Mountain, and Pacific time zones. The states of Alaska and Hawaii are further west than the Pacific time zone. Use a globe to find these two states. What is the time in Alaska and Hawaii if it is 9:00 AM in Los Angeles?

When you cross from one time zone to another, the local time changes by one hour. If you are traveling east, you add one hour for each time zone you cross. If you are traveling west, you subtract one hour for each time zone you cross.

Now suppose you are taking a 24-hour trip around the world. You travel west, leaving Miami, Florida, at 1:00 PM Sunday. Because you are traveling west, you subtract one hour for each time zone you cross. One day later, you arrive back in Miami. It is now 1:00 PM Monday. But because you have subtracted a total of 24 hours as you traveled, you think that it is still 1:00 PM Sunday!

This situation is quite confusing. But geographers have established the **international date line** to simplify matters. The international date line is located

Figure 4-18 *Travelers going west across the international date line gain a day. Those going east across it lose a day. Why does the international date line zigzag?*

along the 180th meridian. When you cross this line going east, you subtract one day. When you cross this line going west, you add one day. So in your trip around the world, you should have added one day, or gone from Sunday to Monday, as you crossed the international date line traveling west. You would then have arrived back in Miami, as expected, at 1:00 PM Monday afternoon.

Parallels

There are also lines from east to west across a map or globe. These lines are called **parallels**. Parallels cross meridians at right angles. The parallel located halfway between the North and South poles is the **equator**. Because parallels run east and west, they measure distance north and south. So in relation to the equator, locations of other parallels are either north or south. The measure of distance north and south of the equator is called **latitude**. Parallels are used to measure latitude.

The equator is labeled 0° latitude. Parallels to the north of the equator are north latitudes. Parallels to the south of the equator are south latitudes. The distance from the equator to either the North or South pole is one quarter of the distance around the Earth.

ACTIVITY DOING

Latitude and Longitude

1. Select ten specific places on the Earth. Use a map or globe and determine the approximate latitude and longitude of each place. For example, if you select New Orleans, Louisiana, your answer will be 30°N, 90°W. If you select Tokyo, Japan, your answer will be 35°N, 140°E.

2. Write down ten random combinations of latitude and longitude. Refer to a map or globe to find the corresponding locations. For example, if you write down 50°S, 70°W, the corresponding location will be southern Argentina.

Why are latitude and longitude important?

Figure 4–19 *Parallels are lines running from east to west on a map or globe. Parallels and meridians form a grid used to determine exact locations. On what continent is 40° north latitude and 90° west longitude located?*

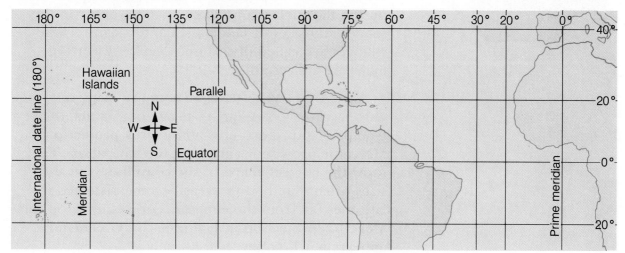

Because one quarter of the distance around a circle is 90°, north and south parallels are labeled from 0° to 90°. The North Pole is at 90° north latitude, or 90°N. The South Pole is at 90° south latitude, or 90°S. Just as there is a meridian for every degree of longitude, there is a parallel for every degree of latitude. But not all parallels are drawn on most globes or maps.

Meridians and parallels form a grid, or network of crossing lines, on a globe or map. They can be used to determine the exact locations east and west of the prime meridian and north and south of the equator. For example, if a ship reported its position as 30° south latitude and 165° east longitude, it would be off the coast of Australia. Why is this system of locating points helpful in shipping?

Types of Maps

Maps of the Earth are very useful. **Maps show locations and distances on the Earth's surface. They also show many different local features. Some maps show the soil types in an area. Some show currents in the ocean. Some maps show small, detailed areas of the Earth. Maps of cities may show every street in those cities.**

However, maps have one serious drawback. Because they are flat, maps cannot represent a round surface accurately. Like a photograph of a person, a map is only a **projection**, or a representation of a three-dimensional object on a flat surface. When the round surface of the Earth is represented on the flat surface of a map, changes occur in the shapes and sizes of landmasses and oceans. These changes are called distortion. Despite distortion, maps are still useful.

MERCATOR PROJECTIONS There are many different ways to project the Earth's image onto a map. One type of map projection is a **Mercator projection**. Mercator projections are used for navigation. They show the correct shape of the coastlines. But the sizes of land and water areas become distorted in latitudes far from the equator. For example, on the Mercator projection in Figure 4–20, Greenland appears much larger than it really is.

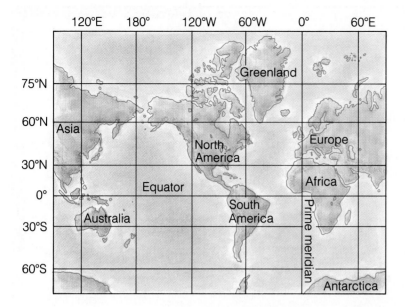

Figure 4–20 *This type of map is called a Mercator projection. What feature of this map is distorted?*

EQUAL-AREA PROJECTIONS   Another type of map projection is called an **equal-area projection**. Equal-area projections show area correctly. The meridians and parallels are placed on the map in such a way that every part of the Earth is the same size on the map as it is on a globe. But the shapes of the areas are distorted on an equal-area projection. What areas in Figure 4–21 look distorted to you?

Figure 4–21 *The correct areas of the Earth's landmasses are shown on this map. But the correct shapes are not. What type of map is this?*

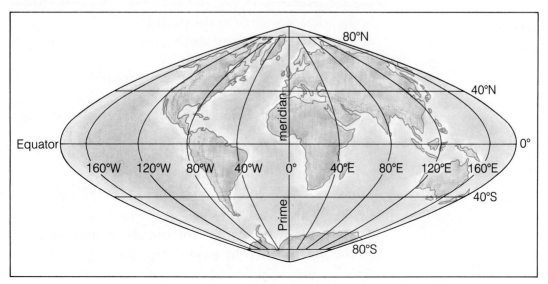

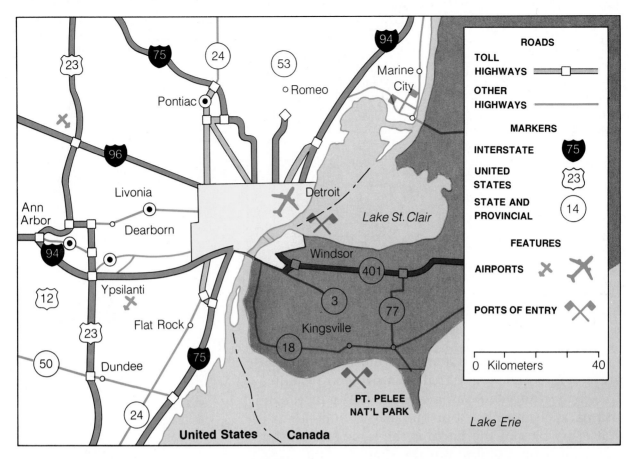

Figure 4-22 *One of the most familiar types of maps is a road map. What kinds of information are provided by the legend of this map?*

4-3 Section Review

1. In what ways are maps useful?
2. Under what circumstances would a globe be more useful than a map?
3. What is a scale? Why is it important?
4. What is longitude? Latitude?
5. What is the international date line? How is this meridian used?
6. What is a time zone? Explain why the Earth has been divided into 24 time zones.
7. What is a projection? What are the two kinds?

Critical Thinking—*Applying Concepts*
8. Why was it important for people to agree on the location of the prime meridian?

PROBLEM Solving

Famous People—Famous Places

Famous people often make places famous. Use the following clues to locate the places on Earth being described. You will need a world atlas to discover the locations.

Interpreting Maps

1. The French artist Gauguin fled Paris to this tropical paradise, whose location is 17°S, 149°W.

2. Marie Curie discovered radium while working in a country whose capital is located at 48.5°N, 2°E.

3. Napoleon spent the last years of his life at 16°S, 5°W.

4. Ponce de Leon found the fountain of youth at 29.5°N, 81°W. The waters, alas, were not all that effective, for he died in 1521.

5. Cecil B. DeMille directed many epic films that were supposed to take place in foreign locations, but which were filmed for the most part at 34°N, 118°W.

6. Betsy Ross was supposed to have sewn the first American flag in this city, located at 40°N, 75°W.

■ Add to this list of famous places by identifying and locating some other important sites. Here are a few examples: where you live; where you were born; where your favorite sports team plays; where you would like to spend a vacation.

Guide for Reading

*Focus on this question as
you read.*

▶ *How do topographic maps
represent features of the
Earth's surface?*

4–4 Topographic Maps

You have learned that the Earth has a varied topography. Perhaps you have even noticed some of the Earth's varied features if you have ever flown in an airplane across the United States. High above the ground, you can easily see mountains, plains, valleys, rivers, lakes, and other features. At ground level, some of these features are more difficult to observe. However, certain types of maps that show even small details of the topography of an area have been drawn. A map that shows the different shapes and sizes of a land surface is called a **topographic map**. This type of map may also show cities, roads, parks, and railroads.

Topographic maps show the relief of the land. Most topographic maps use contour lines to show relief. A **contour line** is a line that passes through all points on a map that have the same elevation. Some topographic maps show relief by using different colors for different elevations.

The difference in elevation from one contour line to the next is called the contour interval. For example, in a map with a contour interval of 5 meters, contour lines are drawn only at elevations of 0 meters, 5 meters, 10 meters, 15 meters, and so on. Look at the contour lines in Figure 4–23. What contour interval is being used here? What is the highest elevation on the hill?

Like other maps, topographic maps use symbols to represent features. Symbols for buildings and roads are usually black. Symbols for bodies of water such as rivers, lakes, and streams are blue. Green represents woods and swamps. And contour lines are brown or red. All symbols on a map are placed in a legend. The legend explains what each symbol represents. See the legend in Figure 4–24 for some common map symbols and their meanings. (Appendix D on page 169 of this textbook contains a more extensive list of map symbols.)

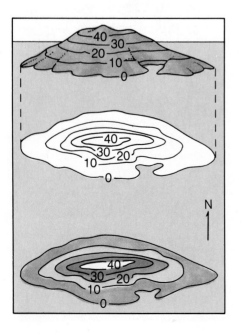

Figure 4–23 *Some topographic maps use colors to indicate different elevations. Others use contour lines to show different elevations.*

TOPOGRAPHIC MAP SYMBOLS

Symbol	Meaning	Symbol	Meaning	Symbol	Meaning
■	House	╪═╪	Bridge	(gravel pattern)	Gravel beach
▙ (flag)	School	┼┼┼┼	Railroad	∿	Contour line
▬▬▬	Primary highway	∼	Perennial stream	(depression symbol)	Depression
====	Unimproved road	(dotted oval)	Dry lake	(swamp symbol)	Swamp

Figure 4–24 *The symbols in this legend are commonly found on topographic maps. What is the symbol for a school? A railroad?*

The first time you look at a topographic map, you may be somewhat confused. All those lines and symbols can seem awesome. But once you become familiar with contour maps and gain experience in interpreting them, a great deal of confusion will be cleared up. The information in a topographic map is quite useful, especially for people who like to hike or who enjoy camping. The following simple rules will make it easier for you to read this type of map:

- A contour line of one elevation never crosses, or intersects, a contour line of another elevation. Each contour line represents only one elevation. Contour lines can never cross because one point cannot have two different elevations.

- Closely spaced contour lines represent a steep slope. The lines are close together because the elevation of a steep slope changes greatly over a short distance. Contour lines spaced far apart represent a gentle slope. The lines are far apart because the elevation of a gentle slope changes only slightly over a short distance.

- Contour lines that cross a valley are V shaped. If a stream flows through the valley, the V will point upstream, or in the direction opposite to the flow of the stream.

ACTIVITY
WRITING

The History of Mapmaking

Using reference materials in the library, write a short essay on the history of mapmaking from the time of the Babylonians to the present. Include information on the following:
Gerhardus Mercator
Christopher Columbus
Claudius Ptolemy
Amerigo Vespucci
Satellite mapping
Include drawings and illustrations with your essay.

■ Contour lines form closed loops around hilltops or depressions. Elevation numbers on the contour lines indicate whether a feature is a hilltop or a depression. If the numbers increase toward the center of the closed loop, the feature is a hilltop. If the numbers decrease, the feature is a depression. Sometimes elevation numbers are not given. Instead short dashes called hachures (HASH-oorz) are used to indicate a depression. Hachures are drawn perpendicular to the contour line that loops around a depression. The hachures point to the inside of the loop.

Now look at Figure 4–25. You should be able to understand all of the information on the map. What is the location of the depression? Which mountain has the steepest slope? In what direction does the Campbell River flow? Now look at Figure 4–26, Figure 4–27 on page 134 and Figure 4–28 on page 135. Use the legend in Figure 4–24 and the rules you have just learned to identify other topographic features.

Figure 4–25 *Once you learn the meanings of map symbols, topographic maps such as this one are easy to read. What does the symbol in green at the bottom of this map represent?*

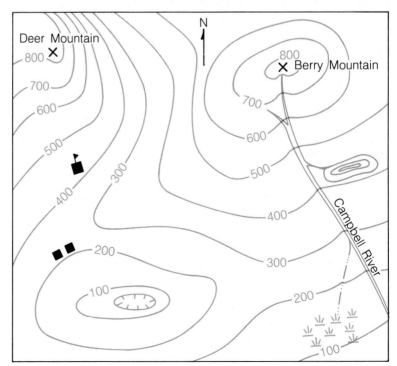

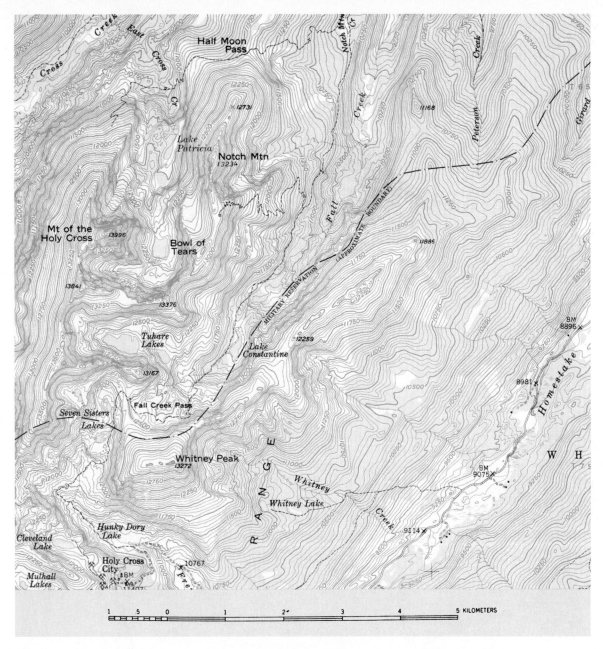

4–4 Section Review

1. How do topographic maps represent features of the Earth's surface?
2. What is a contour line? A contour interval?
3. Why is a map's legend important?

Critical Thinking—*Relating Concepts*
4. Why would it be difficult to show a vertical cliff on a topographic map?

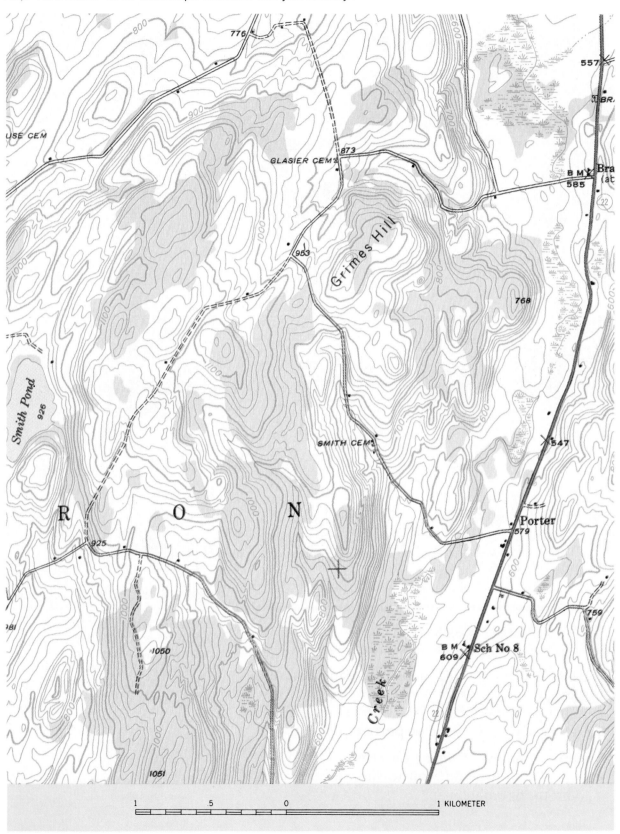

Figure 4–27 *This topographic map shows part of a county in New York State. What landscape features can you identify?*

USE CEM

800

776

GLASIER CEM

873

953

Grimes Hill

768

Smith Pond

926

SMITH CEM

R   O   N

925

1050

1081

1051

Creek

557

BR

B M
585

Bra
(at

22

547

Porter
579

759

B M
609

Sch No 8

22

1   .5   0   1 KILOMETER

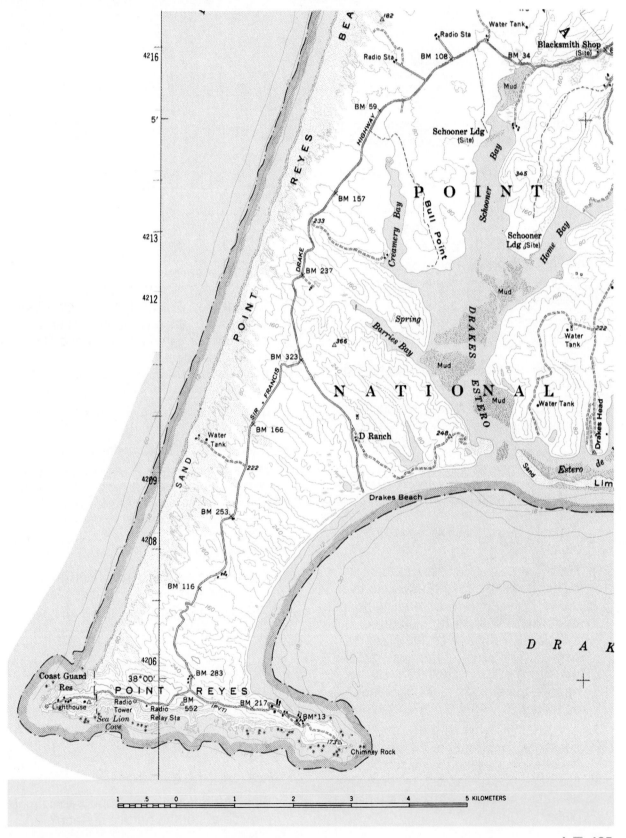

Figure 4-28 *This topographic map shows part of the shoreline of California. What type of landscape region is this area part of?*

Laboratory Investigation

Making a Topographic Map

Problem

What information can a topographic map provide about the surface features of the Earth?

Materials *(per group)*

modeling clay	glass-marking pencil
metric ruler	1 L water
rigid cardboard	pencil
pane of clear glass	sheet of unlined,
aquarium tank or	white paper
deep-sided pan	

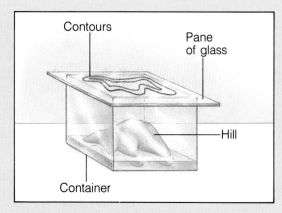

Contours   Pane of glass

Hill

Container

Procedure 🧪

1. Cut the cardboard to fit the bottom of the tank or pan.
2. On top of the cardboard, shape the clay into a model of a hill. Include on the model some gullies, a steep slope, and a gentle slope.
3. When the model is dry and hard, place the model and cardboard into the tank or pan. Pour water into the container to a depth of 1 cm. This will represent sea level.
4. Place the pane of glass over the container. Looking straight down into the container, use the glass-marking pencil to trace the outline of the container on the glass. Also trace on the glass the contour, or outline, of the water around the edges of the model. Carefully remove the pane of glass from the container.
5. Add another centimeter of water to the container. The depth of the water should now be 2 cm. Place the glass in exactly the same position as before. Trace the new contour of the water on the pane of glass.

6. Repeat step 5, adding 1 cm to the depth of the water each time. Stop when the next addition of water would completely cover the model.
7. Remove the pane of glass. With a pencil, trace the contours on the glass onto a sheet of paper. This will be your topographic map.
8. Assume that every centimeter of water you added to the first centimeter (sea level) equals 100 m of elevation on the map. Label the elevation of each contour line on your topographic map.

Observations

1. What is the approximate elevation of the top of the hill?
2. How can you determine if the hill has a steep slope by looking at the contour lines?
3. How can you determine if the hill has a gentle slope by looking at the contour lines?
4. How do contour lines look when they show gullies on the model?

Analysis and Conclusions

What information can a topographic map provide about the Earth's surface?

Study Guide

Summarizing Key Concepts

4–1 The Continents

▲ There are seven continents on Earth: Africa, Antarctica, Asia, Australia, Europe, North America, and South America.

4–2 Topography

▲ The shape of the Earth's surface is called its topography.

▲ The different physical features of an area are called its landscape.

▲ The three main types of landscape regions are mountains, plains, and plateaus.

▲ One characteristic of a landscape region is elevation. The difference in a region's elevations is called its relief.

▲ Mountains have high elevations, and are areas of high relief.

▲ Mountains are usually part of larger groups called mountain ranges, mountain systems, and mountain belts.

▲ Plains are flat land areas that are not far above sea level. They are areas of low relief.

▲ Low, flat areas along the coast are called coastal plains. Low, flat areas found inland are called interior plains.

▲ Plateaus are broad, flat areas that rise more than 600 meters above sea level.

4–3 Mapping the Earth's Surface

▲ A map is a drawing of the Earth, or part of the Earth, on a flat surface. The most accurate representation of the Earth is a globe.

▲ The Earth is divided by lines that run from north to south, called meridians, and by lines that run from east to west, called parallels.

▲ Meridians are used to measure longitude. Parallels are used to measure latitude.

▲ The Earth is divided into 24 time zones.

4–4 Topographic Maps

▲ Topographic maps show the different shapes and sizes of land surfaces.

▲ Topographic maps use contour lines to show relief.

Reviewing Key Terms

Define each term in a complete sentence.

4–1 The Continents
island
continent

4–2 Topography
topography
landscape
elevation
relief
mountain
mountain range
mountain system
mountain belt

plain
coastal plain
interior plain
plateau

4–3 Mapping the Earth's Surface
map
globe
scale
meridian
prime meridian
longitude

time zone
international date line
parallel
equator
latitude
projection
Mercator projection
equal-area projection

4–4 Topographic Maps
topographic map
contour line

Chapter Review

Content Review

Multiple Choice

Choose the letter of the answer that best completes each statement.

1. The smallest landmass that is still considered a continent is
   a. North America. c. Africa.
   b. Australia.   d. Greenland.

2. Large areas of very old, exposed rock that form the core of a continent are called
   a. icecaps.   c. shields.
   b. mountains. d. meridians.

3. Tops of mountains are called
   a. gorges.   c. summits.
   b. elevations. d. projections.

4. Individual mountains are usually
   a. volcanic mountains.
   b. mountain systems.
   c. plateaus.
   d. none of these.

5. The landscape region with the lowest overall elevation is a(an)
   a. mountain belt.   c. plateau.
   b. coastal plain.   d. interior plain.

6. Broad, flat areas of land more than 600 meters above sea level are called
   a. plains.   c. farmland.
   b. plateaus.   d. mountains.

7. The measure of distance east or west of the prime meridian is called
   a. latitude.   c. projection.
   b. parallel.   d. longitude.

8. A map projection that shows the correct shape of coastlines but distorts the sizes of regions far from the equator is called a(an)
   a. Mercator projection.
   b. topographic map.
   c. equal-area projection.
   d. contour projection.

9. Lines on a map that pass through points with the same elevation are called
   a. meridians.   c. parallels.
   b. contour lines.   d. lines of relief.

True or False

If the statement is true, write "true." If it is false, change the underlined word or words to make the statement true.

1. Central America is part of the continent of <u>South America.</u>

2. The three main types of landscape regions are mountains, plains, and <u>continents.</u>

3. <u>Plains</u> are flat areas of land that rise more than 600 meters above sea level.

4. The distance around the world is measured in <u>degrees.</u>

5. The <u>prime meridian</u> divides the parallels of north latitude from those of south latitude.

6. The time in a city one time zone <u>west</u> of another city will be one hour earlier.

Concept Mapping

Complete the following concept map for Section 4–1. Refer to pages I6–I7 to construct a concept map for the entire chapter.

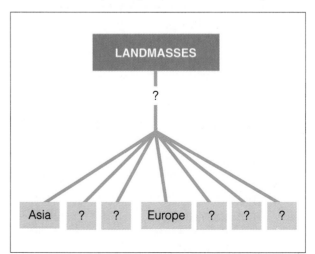

Concept Mastery

Discuss each of the following in a brief paragraph.

1. List the continents. Which continent is also a country? Which continent is almost completely covered by a thick icecap? Which continents are joined to form larger landmasses?
2. How is the topography of an area changed by moving water?
3. Define relief as it relates to Earth's topography. What landscape feature would have high relief? Low relief?
4. What are the similarities and differences between interior plains and coastal plains?
5. Why is the international date line important to travelers?
6. In what ways are maps and globes useful?
7. Why is a map's legend important? What kinds of information can you find in a map's legend?

Critical Thinking and Problem Solving

Use the skills you have developed in this chapter to answer each of the following.

1. **Applying concepts** Explain why the distance measured by degrees of latitude always stays the same, while the distance measured by degrees of longitude varies.
2. **Making predictions** Most of the Earth's ice is found on or around Antarctica. Suppose the temperature of the area around the South Pole climbs above freezing and all of Antarctica's ice melts. Which landscape regions in the rest of the world would be most affected? Why?
3. **Interpreting maps** In Figure 4–27, what contour interval is used? At what elevation is School Number 8? If you wanted to take an easy climb up Grimes Hill, which slope would you choose to climb? Why? Why would you not want to hike in the area located just west of the major highway? Locate the unpaved road west of Grimes Hill. How many kilometers would you walk if you walked from one end of the road to the other? Does the stream flow in or out of Smith Pond? How can you tell?
4. **Relating concepts** Suppose you are the captain of a large ocean liner sailing across the Pacific Ocean from Asia to North America. You notice that the maps in your cabin have the same projection as the map shown in Figure 4–21 on page 127. Are you in trouble? Why?
5. **Applying concepts** You want to go camping with some friends in a national park. You plan to hike into the park on a highway, then leave the road to make your own trails in the forest. How would a road map help you? How would a topographic map of the area help you?
6. **Making maps** Draw topographic maps of three imaginary areas. The first area has a mountain landscape; the second has a plains landscape; the third has several plateaus separated by rivers.
7. **Using the writing process** You are lost in the deep woods with only a scrap of paper, a pencil, a small amount of supplies, and your faithful homing pigeon, Homer. You plan to send Homer for help. Write a note to tie to Homer's leg. Include a map of your location.

Earth's Interior

5

Guide for Reading

After you read the following sections, you will be able to

5–1 The Earth's Core
- ■ Relate the movement of seismic waves to the composition of the Earth's core.
- ■ Describe the characteristics of the inner core and the outer core.

5–2 The Earth's Mantle
- ■ Describe the properties and composition of the mantle.
- ■ Explain what the Moho is.

5–3 The Earth's Crust
- ■ Describe the characteristics of the Earth's crust.
- ■ Compare continental crust and oceanic crust.

In 1864, Jules Verne wrote *Journey to the Center of the Earth*. In this exciting and imaginative tale, Verne describes his idea of what lies hidden beneath the surface of planet Earth.

Verne was not the only person to be fascinated by this unknown world. For many years, scientists have explored the interior of the Earth. But they have not been able to use mechanical probes such as those that explore outer space. The tremendous heat and pressure in the Earth's interior make this region far more difficult to explore than it is to explore planets millions of kilometers away.

In this chapter you will learn about the structure and composition of each layer of the Earth. Afterward, you may want to read *Journey to the Center of the Earth*—and compare Jules Verne's description with the scientific model of the Earth's interior.

Journal *Activity*

You and Your World Have you ever visited a cave or a cavern? If so, in your journal write about your feelings upon first entering the cave's depths. If you have never visited a cave, use your imagination to describe what you think it might be like to walk beneath the surface of the Earth.

◀ *Dangling by what appears to be a slender thread, a group of scientists descend into the Earth.*

What Is the Cause of Earthquakes?

1. Obtain four carpet samples of different colors.

2. Stack the samples on top of one another.

3. Place one hand on each side of the carpet pile and gently press toward the center. Describe what happens.

If the layers of carpet were actually layers of rock, what would happen?

Figure 5–1 *An earthquake in San Francisco twisted and cracked this highway (left). An earthquake in Armenia reduced buildings to rubble (right).*

5–1 The Earth's Core

Scientists use telescopes and space probes to gather information about the planets and the stars. They use microscopes to examine unseen worlds of life on Earth. They use computers and other instruments to gather information about atoms, the building blocks of all matter. So you might find it surprising to learn that most of the information scientists have gathered about the Earth's interior has not come from complex instruments but from earthquakes.

Earthquakes and Seismic Waves

Earthquakes are produced when a part of the Earth's uppermost layer moves suddenly. During an earthquake, the ground shakes and trembles. Sometimes the movement is so violent that buildings crash to the ground and roads and highways are destroyed. Earthquakes produce shock waves that travel through the Earth. These shock waves, which are actually waves of energy, are called **seismic** (SIGHZ-mihk) **waves.** You can make a simple model to show how shock waves move. Fill a sink or basin half full with water and then drop a small pebble onto the center of the water's surface. You will observe waves that move outward from the pebble's point of impact in circles of ever-increasing size.

All earthquakes produce at least two types of seismic waves at the same time: P waves and S waves. These waves are detected and recorded by a special

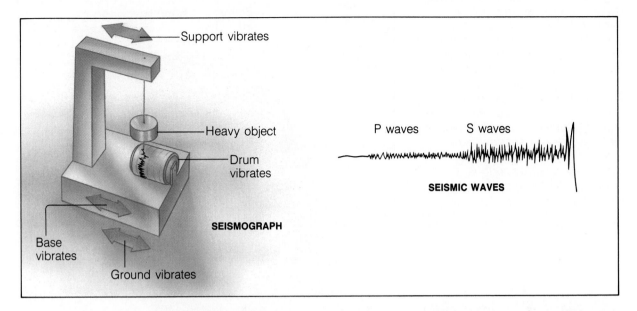

Support vibrates

Heavy object

Drum vibrates

Base vibrates

Ground vibrates

SEISMOGRAPH

P waves   S waves

SEISMIC WAVES

instrument called a **seismograph** (SIGHZ-muh-graf). Figure 5–2 describes what a seismograph looks like and how it works. Seismic waves penetrate the depths of the Earth and return to the surface. During this passage, the speed and direction of the waves change. The changes that occur in the movement of seismic waves are caused by differences in the structure and makeup of the Earth's interior. By recording and studying the waves, scientists have been able to "see" into the interior of the Earth.

Exactly how have P waves and S waves helped scientists develop a model of the Earth's inner structure? At a depth of 2900 kilometers below Earth's surface, P waves passing through the Earth slow down rapidly. S waves disappear. Scientists know that P waves do not move well through liquids and that S waves are stopped completely. So the changes in the movement of the two seismic waves at a depth of 2900 kilometers indicate something significant. Do you know what it is? You are right if you say that 2900 kilometers is the beginning of a liquid layer of the Earth. At a depth of 5150 kilometers, P waves increase their speed. This increase indicates that P waves are no longer traveling through a liquid layer. Instead, P waves are passing through a solid layer of the Earth.

After observing the speeds of P waves and S waves, scientists have concluded that the Earth's center, or core, is actually made up of two layers with different characteristics.

Figure 5–2 *A seismograph (left) detects and records earthquake waves, or seismic waves. A typical pattern of seismic waves is shown (right). What are the two types of seismic waves?*

Figure 5–3 *P waves push together and pull apart rock particles in the direction of the wave movement. The slower S waves move rock particles from side to side at right angles to the wave movement.*

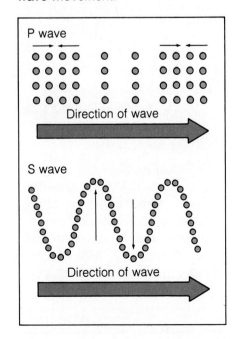

P wave

Direction of wave

S wave

Direction of wave

Figure 5–4 *The paths of seismic waves change as they travel through the Earth. P waves slow down as they pass through the liquid outer core. As they leave the outer core and pass through the inner core, P waves speed up. This change in speed bends the waves. S waves disappear as they enter the outer core. Why? Notice that a wave-free shadow zone extends all the way around the Earth. The shadow zone is produced by the bending of seismic waves.*

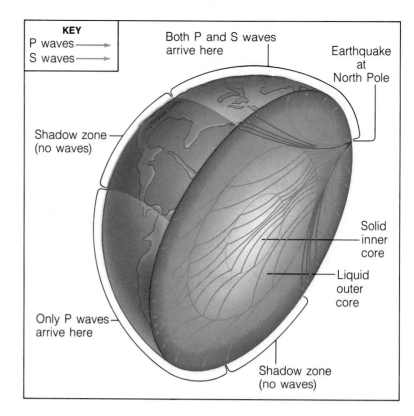

KEY
P waves ——→
S waves ——→

Both P and S waves arrive here

Earthquake at North Pole

Shadow zone (no waves)

Solid inner core

Liquid outer core

Only P waves arrive here

Shadow zone (no waves)

The Earth's Core

Both layers of the Earth's core are made of the elements iron and nickel. The solid, innermost layer is called the **inner core.** Here iron and nickel are under a great deal of pressure. The temperature of the inner core reaches 5000°C. Iron and nickel usually melt at this temperature. The enormous pressure at this depth, however, pushes the particles of iron and nickel so tightly together that the elements remain solid.

The radius, or distance from the center to the edge, of the inner core is about 1300 kilometers. The inner core begins at a depth of about 5150 kilometers below the Earth's surface. The presence of solid iron in the inner core may explain the existence of the magnetic fields around the Earth. Scientists think the iron produces an effect similar to the effect around a magnet—that is, a magnetic field. Have you ever experimented with iron filings and a bar magnet? If so, were you able to observe the pattern of the filings around the magnet? This pattern identifies the magnetic field. Perhaps your teacher can help you do this activity so that you can see a magnetic field for yourself.

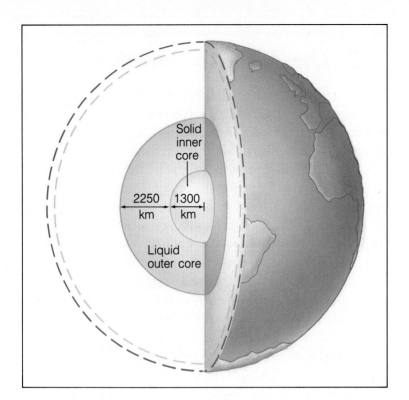

Surrounding the inner core is the second layer of the Earth, called the **outer core.** The outer core begins about 2900 kilometers below the Earth's surface and is about 2250 kilometers thick. The outer core is also made of iron and nickel. In this layer, the temperature ranges from about 2200°C in the upper part to almost 5000°C near the inner core. The heat makes the iron and nickel in the outer core molten, or changed into a hot liquid.

5–1 Section Review

1. What evidence has caused scientists to conclude that the Earth's core is made of two different layers?
2. Name two types of seismic waves. How are these waves the same? How are they different?
3. How are the inner and the outer cores of the Earth alike? How do they differ?

Critical Thinking—*Making Predictions*
4. Predict what would happen to P waves and S waves if the Earth's outer core were solid and its inner core were liquid.

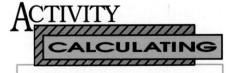

ACTIVITY

CALCULATING

The Speed of Seismic Waves

Some kinds of seismic waves travel at 24 times the speed of sound. The speed of sound is 1250 km/hr. How fast do such seismic waves travel?

5–2 The Earth's Mantle

The layer of the Earth directly above the outer core is the **mantle.** The mantle extends to a depth of about 2900 kilometers below the surface. About 80 percent of the volume of the Earth and about 68 percent of the planet's mass are in the mantle.

In 1909, the Yugoslav scientist Andrija Mohorovičić (moh-hoh-ROH-vuh-chihch) observed a change in the speed of seismic waves as they moved through the Earth. When the waves reached a depth of 32 to 64 kilometers below the Earth's surface, their speed increased. The change in the speed of the waves at this depth indicated a difference in either the density (how tightly together the particles of material are packed) or the composition of the rock. Mohorovičić discovered a boundary between the Earth's outermost layer and the mantle. In his honor, this boundary is now called the **Moho.**

Scientists have made many attempts to determine the composition of the mantle. They have studied rocks from volcanoes because these rocks were formed deep within the Earth. They have also studied rocks from the ocean floor. **After studying rock samples, scientists have determined that the**

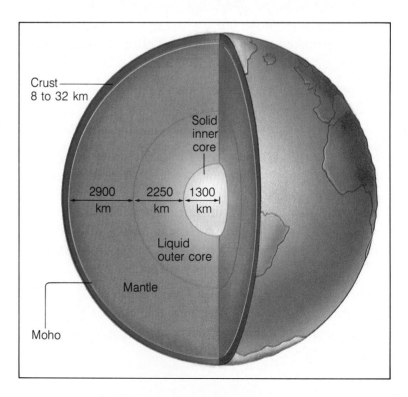

Crust — 8 to 32 km

Solid inner core

2900 km 2250 km 1300 km

Liquid outer core

Mantle

Moho

Figure 5–6 *The mantle is the Earth's layer that lies above the outer core. The crust is only a very thin layer of the Earth. Most of the crust is covered with soil, rock, and water. What is the name of the boundary between the mantle and the crust?*

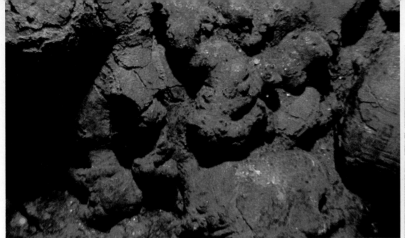

mantle is made mostly of the elements silicon, oxygen, iron, and magnesium. The lower mantle has a greater percentage of iron than the upper mantle has.

The density of the mantle increases with depth. This increase in density is perhaps due to the greater percentage of iron in the lower mantle. The temperature and the pressure within the mantle also increase with depth. The temperature ranges from 870°C in the upper mantle to about 2200°C in the lower mantle.

Studies of seismic waves suggest that the rock in the mantle can flow like a thick liquid. The high temperature and pressure in the mantle allow the solid rock to flow slowly, thus changing shape. When a solid has the ability to flow, it has the property of **plasticity** (plas-TIHS-uh-tee).

Figure 5–7 *Kilauea is an active volcano in Hawaii. Here you can see lava being thrown into the air as the volcano erupts (right). Lava, either from a volcano or from a rift valley in the ocean floor, forms these "pillow" shapes when it is rapidly cooled by ocean water (left).*

5–2 Section Review

1. What elements make up most of the mantle?
2. Where is the mantle located? How far does it extend below the Earth's surface?
3. What is the Moho?
4. What is plasticity?

Connection—*You and Your World*

5. In areas where earthquakes are common, the foundations of buildings are constructed so that they can move slightly on special slippery pads. Architects believe that these buildings will not be damaged during an earthquake. How would this type of construction make a building safer during an earthquake?

ACTIVITY

DOING

A Model of the Earth's Interior

1. Obtain a Styrofoam ball 15 cm or more in diameter.

2. Carefully cut out a wedge from the ball so that the ball is similar to the one in Figure 5–6.

3. Draw lines on the inside of the ball and on the inside of the wedge to represent the four layers of the Earth.

4. Label and color each layer on the ball and wedge.

Guide for Reading

Focus on these questions as you read.
▶ *What is the Earth's crust?*
▶ *How does oceanic crust compare with continental crust?*

Figure 5–8 *Natural rock formations, such as these in Big Bend National Park, Texas, often take beautiful, and sometimes surprising, forms. The elements that make up the Earth's crust are listed in this chart. What two elements are the most abundant?*

ELEMENTS IN THE EARTH'S CRUST

Element	Percentage in Crust
Oxygen	46.60
Silicon	27.72
Aluminum	8.13
Iron	5.00
Calcium	3.63
Sodium	2.83
Potassium	2.59
Magnesium	2.09
Titanium	0.40
Hydrogen	0.14
Total	99.13

5–3 The Earth's Crust

The Earth's crust is its thin outermost layer. The **crust** is much thinner than the mantle and the outer and inner cores. You can think of the crust as being similar to the peel on an apple. All life on Earth exists on or within a few hundred meters above the crust. Most of the crust cannot be seen. Do you know why? It is covered with soil, rock, and water. There is one place, however, where the crust can be seen. Where do you think that might be?

The crust is made of three types of solid rocks: igneous rocks, sedimentary rocks, and metamorphic rocks. Igneous rocks form when hot liquid rock from deep within the Earth cools and hardens as it reaches the surface. The word igneous means "born of fire," a term that explains with accuracy how these rocks are formed. Sedimentary rocks form when sediments—small pieces of rocks, sand, and other materials—are pressed and cemented together by the weight of layers that build up over long periods of time. Metamorphic rock forms when igneous and sedimentary rocks are changed by heat, pressure, or the action of chemicals.

The thickness of the Earth's crust varies. Crust beneath the oceans, called oceanic crust, is less than 10 kilometers thick. Its average thickness is only about 8 kilometers. Oceanic crust is made mostly of silicon, oxygen, iron, and magnesium.

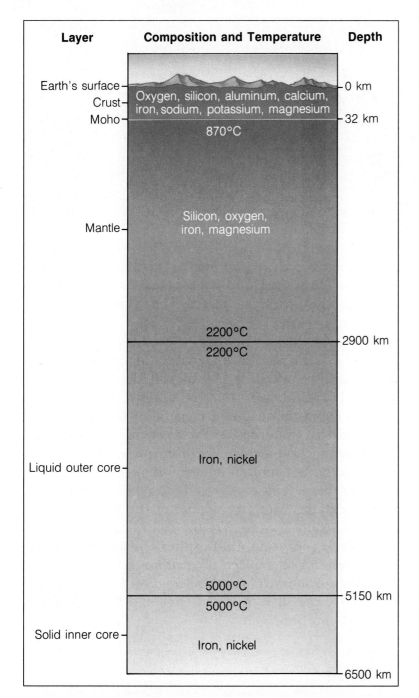

Layer	Composition and Temperature	Depth
Earth's surface	Oxygen, silicon, aluminum, calcium, iron, sodium, potassium, magnesium	0 km
Crust		
Moho	870°C	32 km
Mantle	Silicon, oxygen, iron, magnesium	
	2200°C	2900 km
Liquid outer core	2200°C Iron, nickel	
	5000°C	5150 km
Solid inner core	5000°C Iron, nickel	6500 km

Figure 5–9 *This diagram summarizes the major characteristics of the Earth's layers. Which layers are solid? Which layer is liquid?*

Activity Bank

How Hard Is That Rock?, p.172

ACTIVITY
CALCULATING

How Many Earths?

The distance from the center of the Earth to the surface is about 6450 kilometers. The distance from the Earth to the sun is 150 million kilometers. How many Earths lined up in a row are needed to reach the sun?

Crust beneath the continents, called continental crust, has an average thickness of about 32 kilometers. Beneath mountains, continental crust is much thicker. Under some mountains, the crust's thickness is greater than 70 kilometers. Continental crust is made mostly of silicon, oxygen, aluminum, calcium, sodium, and potassium.

The Earth's crust forms the upper part of the **lithosphere** (LIHTH-uh-sfeer). The lithosphere is the

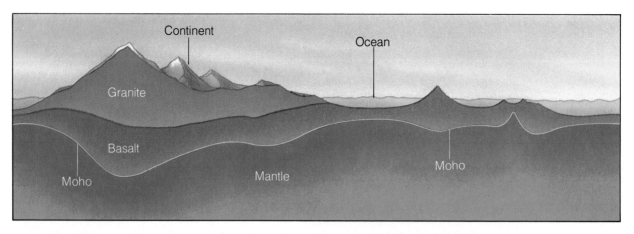

Figure 5–10 *The Earth's crust consists of two layers. The top layer is made of granite and is found only under the continents. The bottom layer is made of basalt and is found under both the continents and the oceans.*

CAREERS

Geologist

People who study the structure, composition, and history of the Earth are called **geologists.** Geologists spend some of their time examining rocks and other structures in the crust. Geologists usually specialize in a particular area of geology. To learn more about this field, write to the American Geological Institute, 5202 Leesburg Pike, Falls Church, VA 22041.

solid topmost part of the Earth. It is between 50 and 100 kilometers thick and is broken up into large sections called lithospheric plates. There are at least seven major plates.

The layer directly beneath the lithosphere is called the **asthenosphere** (az-THEEN-oh-sfeer). The asthenosphere, which is 130 to 160 kilometers thick, is actually considered to be the upper edge of the mantle. The asthenosphere is made of hot, molten material. This material has the property of plasticity and thus can flow easily. The lithospheric plates move on the hot molten material that forms the asthenosphere. You can get a better idea of this concept by making your own model of the lithosphere and the asthenosphere. Try the following: Use a slice of bread to represent a lithospheric plate and a layer of jelly spread on a piece of cardboard to represent the asthenosphere. Place the bread on top of the jelly. Move the slice of bread back and forth slightly. What do you observe?

5–3 Section Review

1. What is the Earth's crust?
2. Compare oceanic crust with continental crust.
3. What are the characteristics of the asthenosphere? What floats on this layer?

Critical Thinking—*Relating Concepts*
4. Explain why metamorphic rock could not form before igneous or sedimentary rock.

CONNECTIONS

Beauty From Beneath the Earth's Surface

The Smithsonian Institution in Washington, D.C., has often been called the nation's attic. But you should not think of a dusty attic filled with unwanted and unused objects. For the Smithsonian Institution is a treasure-filled attic: a storehouse of items of great artistic merit made by talented women and men, as well as of treasures from the Earth itself. Here you will find diamonds, rubies, sapphires, and other gems valuable beyond price—all handcrafted by the forces of nature in a "laboratory" you know as the Earth.

For example, scientists believe that diamonds form within the upper part of the Earth's mantle. Here the pressure is tremendous—about 65,000 times the pressure at the Earth's surface—and the temperature is close to 1500°C! Under these extreme conditions of pressure and temperature, carbon can be transformed into diamonds. Diamond-laden molten rock is forced to the surface of the Earth by volcanic explosions. Mines cut into the crust expose the diamonds formed long ago in the Earth's mantle. These rough diamonds vary in quality. Those that are gem quality are cut and shaped into precious stones used in jewelry. Those that are not fine enough to be made into jewelry are used to make drills and saws. Such *industrial-grade diamonds* are so strong that they cut through many materials, including steel. Small bits of diamond are often used in the dental drills that remove decayed parts of teeth and in the needles that follow the grooves in a record to produce the sounds of music.

If you are able to visit the Smithsonian Institution at some future time, keep this in mind: Not all the great treasures preserved and protected within the walls of this great museum were made by the hands of people; many were shaped by forces at work deep within the Earth.

Gemstones, like this green beryl, are quite beautiful. Diamonds, highly valued for their beauty, also have important uses in industry. Small diamond particles are often imbedded in drills (left) and in saws (right).

Laboratory Investigation

Simulating Plasticity

Problem

How can the plasticity of the Earth's mantle be simulated?

Materials *(per group)*

15 g cornstarch
2 small beakers
10 mL cold water
medicine dropper
metal stirring rod or spoon

Procedure 🧪

1. Put 15 g of cornstarch in one of the beakers. Into the other beaker, pour 10 mL of cold water.

2. Use the medicine dropper to gradually add one dropperful of water to the cornstarch. Stir the mixture.

3. Continue to add the water, one dropperful at a time. Stir the mixture after each addition. Stop adding the water when the mixture becomes difficult to stir.

4. Try to pour the mixture into your hand. Try to roll the mixture into a ball and press it.

Observations

1. Before the addition of water, is the cornstarch a solid, liquid, or gas? Is the water a solid, liquid, or gas?

2. When you try to pour the mixture into your hand, does the mixture behave like a solid, liquid, or gas?

3. When you try to roll the mixture into a ball and apply pressure, does the mixture act like a solid, liquid, or gas?

Analysis and Conclusions

1. How is the mixture of cornstarch and water similar to the Earth's mantle? Different from the Earth's mantle?

2. How might the plasticity of the mantle influence the movement of the Earth's lithospheric plates?

3. **On Your Own** Make a model of a lithospheric plate. Devise a way to show how the plasticity of the mantle allows the Earth's lithospheric plates to move.

Study Guide

Summarizing Key Concepts

5–1 The Earth's Core

▲ An earthquake is a sudden movement of the Earth's outermost layer.

▲ Shock waves produced by an earthquake are called seismic waves.

▲ Seismic waves are detected and recorded by an instrument called a seismograph.

▲ Seismic waves called P waves and S waves are used to study the structure and composition of the Earth's interior.

▲ The core of the Earth is made of a liquid outer core and a solid inner core. Both core layers are composed of iron and nickel.

▲ Although the temperature is high enough to melt iron and nickel, the inner core is solid because of the enormous pressure.

▲ The dense iron and nickel in the inner core may be the cause of the Earth's magnetic field.

▲ The temperature range of the Earth's outer core is from about 2200°C to almost 5000°C.

▲ P waves do not move very well through liquids. S waves do not move through liquids at all. This information has helped scientists determine that the outer core is liquid and the inner core is solid.

5–2 The Earth's Mantle

▲ The mantle is the layer of the Earth that lies above the outer core.

▲ The mantle makes up about 80 percent of the Earth's volume and 68 percent of the Earth's mass.

▲ The boundary between the Earth's outermost layer and the mantle is called the Moho.

▲ The mantle is made mostly of silicon, oxygen, iron, and magnesium.

▲ Pressure and temperature increase with depth in the mantle.

▲ Because of the tremendous heat and pressure in the mantle, rocks in the mantle exhibit the property of plasticity.

5–3 The Earth's Crust

▲ The crust is the thin outermost layer of the Earth.

▲ The crust is made of igneous, sedimentary, and metamorphic rocks.

▲ The most abundant elements in the crust are oxygen, silicon, aluminum, iron, calcium, sodium, potassium, and magnesium.

▲ Oceanic crust is about 8 kilometers thick. Continental crust is about 32 kilometers thick.

▲ The crust forms the upper part of the lithosphere. The lithosphere contains large sections called lithospheric plates.

▲ Lithospheric plates move about on the asthenosphere, the outermost edge of the mantle. The asthenosphere exhibits the property of plasticity.

Reviewing Key Terms

Define each term in a complete sentence.

5–1 The Earth's Core
seismic waves
seismograph
inner core
outer core

5–2 The Earth's Mantle
mantle
Moho
plasticity

5–3 The Earth's Crust
crust
lithosphere
asthenosphere

Chapter Review

Content Review

Multiple Choice

Choose the letter of the answer that best completes each statement.

1. The shock waves produced by an earthquake are measured with a
   a. radiograph.   c. sonograph.
   b. seismograph.   d. laser.
2. The Earth's inner core is made of
   a. oxygen and silicon.
   b. iron and nickel.
   c. iron and silicon.
   d. copper and nickel.
3. The boundary between the mantle and the outermost layer of the Earth is called the
   a. Moho.   c. lithosphere.
   b. outer core.   d. bedrock.
4. The crust of the Earth is made mostly of
   a. oxygen and silicon.
   b. iron and silicon.
   c. iron and nickel.
   d. copper and nickel.
5. When P waves and S waves reach the Earth's outer core,
   a. both keep moving at the same speed.
   b. both stop completely.
   c. P waves stop and S waves slow down.
   d. S waves stop and P waves slow down.
6. The layer that makes up most of the Earth's mass and volume is the
   a. mantle.   c. crust.
   b. magma.   d. core.
7. The ability of a solid to flow is called
   a. ductility.   c. seismology.
   b. plasticity.   d. porosity.
8. The thin outermost layer of the Earth is called the
   a. mantle.   c. crust.
   b. Moho.   d. core.

True or False

If the statement is true, write "true." If it is false, change the underlined word or words to make the statement true.

1. The <u>atmosphere</u> is the outermost layer of the mantle on which the plates move.
2. The innermost layer of the Earth is called the <u>inner</u> core.
3. The outer core is <u>molten</u>.
4. <u>S waves</u> slow down as they pass <u>through</u> liquids.
5. The outermost layer of the Earth is called the <u>crust</u>.
6. The topmost solid part of the Earth is broken up into <u>lithospheric plates</u>.
7. The presence of <u>copper</u> in the inner core may explain the <u>magnetic</u> field that exists around the Earth.

Concept Mapping

Complete the following concept map for Section 5–1. Refer to pages I6–I7 to construct a concept map for the entire chapter.

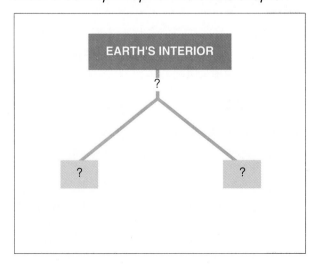

Concept Mastery

Discuss each of the following in a brief paragraph.

1. How have scientists learned about the composition of the Earth's interior?
2. How does oceanic crust differ from continental crust?
3. How do temperature and pressure change as you move from the Earth's crust to the inner core? How do temperature and pressure affect the properties of materials found in the Earth?
4. Briefly describe the work of Andrija Mohorovičić. What did this scientist discover?
5. What is igneous rock? Sedimentary rock? Metamorphic rock?
6. How does the property of plasticity shown by the asthenosphere account for the movement of lithospheric plates?

Critical Thinking and Problem Solving

Use the skills you have developed in this chapter to answer each of the following.

1. **Analyzing data** The temperature of the inner core reaches about 5000°C. The temperature of the outer core begins at 2200°C. Explain why the outer core is liquid and the inner core is solid.
2. **Relating concepts** It has been said that "Every cloud has a silver lining." What could be the "silver lining" in an earthquake?
3. **Analyzing illustrations** This illustration shows the layers of the Earth. Something is wrong with this artist's ideas, however. Identify the errors and describe what you would do to correct them.

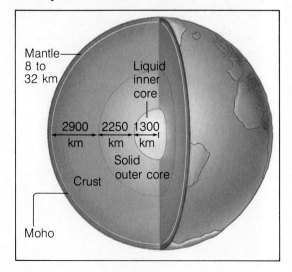

4. **Making models** Use the information in this chapter to make a model of the four layers of the Earth's interior. You may use clay of different colors, papier-mâché, or other materials to make your model. Keep the depth and thickness of each layer of your model in scale with the actual depth and thickness of the Earth's layers. Include a key to the scale you use to construct your model. For example, 1 centimeter in your model might equal 1000 kilometers in the Earth.
5. **Interpreting diagrams** Look at Figure 5–4 on page 144. You will notice an area of the Earth labeled the shadow zone. Use this diagram and your knowledge of seismic waves and the structure of the Earth's interior to explain what the shadow zone is.
6. **Using the writing process** Write a short story about an imaginary trip taken in a machine that is able to drill through the Earth. Make your destination an exotic country on the side of the Earth opposite the city or town in which you live. Use a globe to help. You might like to illustrate this story with appropriate pictures.

GAZETTE

Alan Kolata & Oswaldo Rivera

THE MYSTERIOUS CANALS OF BOLIVIA

The Pampa Koani, a treeless plain in northern Bolivia, was rich in strange ridges and depressions but poor in crops. The Aymara Indians, the inhabitants of this flood plain, were forced to watch as their crops succumbed to frost and their potatoes rotted in the boggy soil. The Aymara knew that nearly one thousand years ago their ancestors had farmed the land successfully. That powerful pre-Incan civilization, called the Tiwanaku state, had flourished from 200 to 1000 AD. What farming methods did the Tiwanakus know so many years ago that the Aymara lacked today?

In 1981, two archaeologists suggested a possible answer. Alan Kolata (bottom left), a professor of archaeology and anthropology at the University of Chicago, and Oswaldo Rivera (bottom right), an archaeologist at Bolivia's National Institute of Archaeology, had been studying the Tiwanaku culture since the late 1970s. The two scholars believed that the secret lay in the ridges and ruts that ran across the flood plain. They had observed similar topographical patterns in Mayan and Aztec farming sites in the jungles of Central America. The archaeologists suggested that the patterns were part of a sophisticated system of canals and raised planting surfaces that had allowed the Tiwanakus to grow their crops successfully.

Kolata and Rivera needed to test their hypothesis. A proven, correct theory would be more than simply a credit to the archaeologists' research abilities. It would also be

a way to rejuvenate the failing Aymara farms and produce hardy crops. In 1981, the archaeologists' first attempt to rehabilitate the Aymara fields was met with a severe drought. It was not until 1987 that Kolata and Rivera were able to convince the Aymara to try again. At first, only one man agreed to cooperate. As a result, he was scorned by his neighbors, who thought the archaeologists were meddling foreigners who would only harm Aymara agriculture. The Aymaras continued to plant their crops away from the rutted fields on nearby hillsides. But the archaeologists and the lone Aymara farmer persevered. Together, the three redug the channels, planted the potato crop, and watched excitedly as the plants grew to record heights.

Then, only a few days before the first harvest, frost struck the area. The Aymara farmers looked on helplessly as 90 percent of their hillside crops were lost. They expected the same fate for the crops Kolata and Rivera had helped to cultivate. The coldest, heaviest air, they thought, would flow downhill onto the flood plain, killing every plant.

The archaeologists hoped for a different outcome. And indeed, when they went out before dawn to investigate, they beheld a remarkable sight! Across the entire flood plain, a white mist lay like a blanket over the potato crops. With the first rays of sunlight, the mist disappeared, revealing undamaged potato plants. Almost the entire crop had survived the killing frost! It was then that Kolata and Rivera, along with the Aymara farmers, recognized the ingenuity of the early Tiwanakus. These ancient people knew how to use the system of canals and ridges to protect their harvest. Can you guess how they did it?

During the day, the soil absorbs heat from the sun. But the soil quickly loses its warmth during the cold night, putting the crops at risk. Water, however, retains heat for a much longer time than soil does. A temperature difference between the water in the canals and the air causes the water to evaporate. This causes a protective, blanketlike mist to form over the crops. In addition, warm water is drawn by capillary action into the

▲ **These Bolivian farmers are harvesting potatoes produced in raised fields bordered by canals.**

raised platforms, conducting warmth into the soil and into the plants' root systems.

Kolata and Rivera were pleased with their discovery—and particularly with the fact that the Aymara began to trust them and treat them like friends. But nobody was more pleased than the Aymara people themselves. With the "new" farming system, their crops began to prosper, yielding bountiful harvests of potatoes, barley, oats, lettuce, and onions. As a bonus, algae and nitrogen-fixing bacteria began to thrive in the canals, providing a useful source of fertilizer after the crops were harvested and the canals were drained. And the Aymara had done all this by returning to the ways of their ancestors!

Meanwhile, Kolata and Rivera continue to research the Tiwanaku culture, which reached its peak in 600 AD. They are especially interested in the daily life of the Tiwanaku people—what they ate, what they wore, and how their society was structured. With a team that includes hydrologists and computer scientists, they study the sophisticated Tiwanaku temples and pyramids as well as their canal system. But Kolata and Rivera are just as interested in the present as in the past. The raised-field technology they helped the Aymara to implement can be used in other areas of Bolivia to help feed a hungry population.

Who Gives a Hoot for the Spotted Owl?

▲ Logging in the old growth forests in the Pacific Northwest threatens the survival of this pair of northern spotted owls.

It is the still of the night in the Pacific Coast's Cascade Mountain range. A small owl swoops out of the upper reaches of a Douglas fir tree, taking advantage of the dark to find its dinner. This bird, the northern spotted owl, is a delicate creature, shy of the daylight and of too much human attention. But recently, it has been forced into the middle of an environmental controversy.

The controversy centers on the logging industry in the Pacific Northwest, for the spotted owl's natural habitat is also a prime source of commercial timber. A century of logging has removed roughly 90 percent of the region's ancient trees. Firs, pines, cedars, and oaks—all at least 250 years old—make up "old-growth" forests. In the process of harvesting wood necessary for houses, buildings, and paper products, the logging industry has also cleared away trees that are the home of the spotted owl. As its habitat dwindled, so did the bird's numbers. The result: a clash between conservationists concerned with the survival of the owl and the logging industry concerned with its employees and its profitability.

In the early 1990s, after much discussion, the United States Fish and Wildlife Service declared the bird a threatened species. This government agency also adopted plans to limit logging in the old-growth areas in order to protect the owl's habitat. Up until that time, the United States Forest Service, which is responsible for overseeing America's forests, had been selling the equivalent of 12 billion board feet of lumber a year to logging companies. That is equal to about 400,000 acres of forest and $1.5 billion. Today, restrictions protect some 50,000 of these acres a year. But conservationists argue that this is not enough. They want the United States Government to exert even tighter controls on the timber industry to protect the owl's habitat. Logging officials claim that environmentalists are exaggerating the threat to the bird.

Although much national attention is focused on the plight of one specific (and cute) creature, it is not simply the owl that is at stake in the debate over logging. At stake, say some ecologists and conservationists, is nothing less than an entire forest ecosystem. At stake, say some officials in the timber industry, is nothing less than 30,000 jobs and the economies of Oregon, Washington State, and northern California. The debate over the spotted owl, then, is really a debate about the role of people and their responsibility for the Earth's environments.

Old-growth forests contain tremendous ecological diversity. The ancient trees used as lumber play an essential role in preserving that ecosystem. They provide a home for a large number of different insect, bird, mammal, and plant species. They also play an important role in cleaning the air and in conserving soil and water in the forest. Moisture on the trees' leaves helps trap dust and other particles to cleanse the air. Root systems absorb water and prevent runoff and soil erosion.

Finally, fallen logs and needles provide the soil with rich nutrients to nourish young tree seedlings and other forest plants.

But the old-growth trees play an important role in the economy. Bark and sawdust from the huge trees are used as fuel to generate electricity and produce particle board. Lumber is used for a variety of construction purposes. And pulp, which is wood from a layer just inside the bark, is used to make a variety of paper products. Finally, this industry represents hundreds of thousands of jobs in the Pacific Northwest and billions of dollars in income.

Logging officials say that they have been respectful of the environment they have a right to use. In fact, it is in their best interests, they say, to protect the trees that quite literally feed and house them. They add that they are careful to replace the trees they have harvested. Because of reforestation, they say, they have reduced the number of trees in the area by only 25 percent, not 90 percent. Logging officials also argue that the logging industry in the United States meets important demands of the entire industrialized world. They say that strict limitations on logging will cost some 30,000 jobs and hundreds of millions of dollars in the coming decade.

But conservationists say the timber industry does much more harm than good. They fear that the industry has overstepped "natural" bounds and rights in its cutting down of the forests. Reforestation, they explain, cannot replace the old-growth trees that foresters

▼ Standing tall and true, these trees are home for many organisms. They are also a source of jobs and lumber for people.

▲ On the ground, cut trees are the promise of paper and lumber. ▶ From the air, you can see how clear-cutting lumber produces a new environment. What effects does harvesting lumber in this way have on the environment?

cut. Loggers may replant trees, but they cannot replace the old-growth ecosystem and its diversity. They also argue that the logging industry is recklessly abusing the environment, as well as destroying itself—it will use up harvestable forest land in 30 years.

Caught in the midst of this conflict are the people of the Pacific Northwest. They want to respect nature's bounty that surrounds them, but many of them are dependent upon the logging industry for their livelihoods. For them, it is not necessarily a philosophical question of the place of humans in the environment. It is a question of food on their tables and clothes for their children.

One compromise that appeals to a variety of groups is a different kind of logging called "New Forestry." Conventional logging techniques use the "clear-cut" method. Clear-cutting removes all the trees in swatches of about 40 acres. From the air, regions of the Pacific Northwest look like a huge checkerboard made of cleared and uncleared areas of trees. New Forestry offers a different approach. Instead of cutting all the trees in a

small area, the new method proposes to harvest larger areas, leaving 20 to 70 percent of the trees standing. The plan also demands that loggers leave some cut trunks on the floor of the forest to add nutrients to the soil and to provide food for plants and animals. According to ecologists, New Forestry techniques resemble ways that forests are affected by natural catastrophes such as forest fires. By leaving a large portion of the trees in a given area still standing, scientists hope to protect and preserve the health and diversity of the forests.

Both the logging industry and environmentalists have expressed concerns about New Forestry, however. Timber officials say that this new method is costly and less effective than clear-cutting. They also say that any change is unnecessary at this time. Conservationists argue that the plan does not offer a complete solution to the problems of logging, but instead detracts attention from these problems. Do you think there can be a "complete resolution" to this debate over logging?

CITIES UNDER THE SEA

"Oh no," I groaned, "that ends our plans for surfacing."

I gazed sadly at the three-dimensional image that floated in the middle of my room. The picture my holovision produced showed towering waves and sheets of falling rain. The voice of the weather forecaster could be heard describing the violent storm that raged 70 meters above my head. The "weather" where I lived was, of course, perfectly calm. It al-ways was since the effects of storms disap-pear just a few meters below the sea's sur-face.

"Off," I said sharply to the control com-puter, taking my anger and disappointment out on the machine.

"Now what?" I thought. As if in answer to my question, the communications system chimed.

"Yes?" I said as I eagerly turned toward the computer console.

My friend Willie's image appeared on the screen. "I guess we're not going to picnic on an island after all," she said. "Disappointed?"

"Of course. I've been to the surface only a few times. I was really looking forward to today's trip, in spite of what's up there: the danger of sunlight to my skin and eyes, air pollution, storms, hot days and cold ones."

"Well cheer up," Willie quickly replied. "Old Professor Melligrant has another plan in mind. She's going to take us to the site of a wreck. It's many kilometers from here, so we're going to use scooters. Grab your gill and get going!"

PREPARING FOR TRAVEL

With my spirits high at the thought of an adventure, I slipped on my water suit. It felt stiff and warm while I remained in my underwater home. But I knew I'd appreciate its warmth and protection in the cool watery world outside. Then I reached into a drawer for my goggles and the all-important gill. I looked at the thin membrane that would fit comfortably over my nose and mouth. And I marveled that such a small, simple device could enable a person to work and travel for countless hours under water.

The material the gill is made of contains proteins. These proteins separate oxygen from water. And we breathe the oxygen. The gill material is used in many ways throughout our underwater city—in our homes, work stations, and transportation vehicles—to provide oxygen for breathing. Without it, human cities beneath the sea would be impossible.

Dressed in my water suit and holding my gill and goggles, I pressed a button that would call a transporter. Seconds later, a blue lamp glowed above the door. My vehicle had arrived. When the door opened, I stepped into the car and pressed the button that indicated where I wanted to go. Whizzing through the transparent tubes that linked various parts of the underwater city, I could see dozens of other cars moving in one direction or another.

At last my car pulled into the transport station located next to the great dome of our school. Professor Melligrant and nine students were already at the school. Melligrant waved me over.

I couldn't help laughing to myself when I saw John. In addition to the usual gear everyone was wearing for this trip, John was loaded down with camera, lights, sonic probe, and a long-range communicator. The sonic probe, which he held in his hand, gave off sounds that could be heard by fish, but not by humans. It was often used to round up or drive away fish. The long-range communicator would come in handy if our little group of explorers got into trouble far from home.

Professor Melligrant unfolded a large map. As we clustered around, she pointed to the general area of the wreck. We walked to the school's exit chamber, a room that would fill with water when we were ready to go. In the dimness of the exit chamber, our suits glowed. So did the water scooters parked nearby. Both the suits and scooters contain materials that react chemically with sea water and give off light. So it would be easy to spot our band of adventurers in the darkness of the ocean.

EXPLORING THE DEPTHS

When everyone was finally ready, the switches were flipped and water flooded into the exit chamber. We turned on the engines of our scooters and followed Professor Melligrant out into the open ocean. After traveling about 1 kilometer, the lights of the city's power station came into view. From the ocean floor, the station rises almost to the surface of the water. Here electricity is generated for the entire city. And at a nearby station, some of that electricity is used to separate hydrogen from water. The hydrogen is used as fuel.

Next came the farms. Although we could not see them, we knew that sonic fences surrounded the area. These invisible fences send out sounds that fish can hear. The fish do not pass through these sound fences. And as a result, huge schools of fish remain penned in fish farms. As we passed by, a lone herder waved to us. Just a short distance away, flashing lights indicated the location of thick wire cables. At the top of these cables, which extended to just below the ocean surface, are the huge kelp beds. Kelp, a kind of seaweed, is an important food substance. And kelp farming is a popular occupation.

A few kilometers beyond the kelp farms, we came across the first signs of seabed mining. According to the older inhabitants of our city, the prospect of seabed mining had first brought people to live under the sea. Robot miners, which looked like big horseshoe crabs, slowly moved along the sea floor scooping up lumps of the metals titanium and manganese.

Beyond the mining area were several large canyons, which we speedily crossed. Then, as we approached an extremely wide canyon, Professor Melligrant's scooter slowed down. She turned to the right and gradually descended. We followed.

The searchlight beam on Professor Melligrant's scooter probed the canyon floor. Then it came to a stop at what looked like a big rock. We had reached the wreck. We parked our scooters around it. Our searchlights brightened the whole area.

Professor Melligrant had never told us exactly what type of ship the wreck was. So I had expected to see the funnels and decks of an old oceanliner. Instead, what I gazed at was part of a sausage-shaped object covered with sea organisms.

Using a portable communicator, Professor Melligrant explained to us that the wreck was a submarine of the twentieth century. In this type of vehicle, people without gills had ventured beneath the surface of the sea.

Unlike other explorers of the deep, the people in this submarine had not come in peace. But that had been long, long ago. Today, the only enemy a person can find under water is a curious shark. And it can quickly be sent swimming away with the silent toot of a sonic probe.

For Further Reading

If you have been intrigued by the concepts examined in this textbook, you may also be interested in the ways fellow thinkers—novelists, poets, essayists, as well as scientists—have imaginatively explored the same ideas.

Chapter 1: Earth's Atmosphere

Carson, Rachel. *Silent Spring*. Boston, MA: Houghton Mifflin.

Randolph, Blythe. *Amelia Earhart*. New York: Watts.

Seuss, Dr. *The Lorax*. New York: Random House.

Silverstein, Alvin, and Virginia B. Silverstein. *Allergies*. Philadelphia, PA: Lippincott.

Verne, Jules. *Around the World in Eighty Days*. New York: Bantam Books.

Verne, Jules. *From the Earth to the Moon*. New York: Airmont.

Young, Louise B. *Sowing the Wind: Reflections on the Earth's Atmosphere*. New York: Prentice Hall Press.

Chapter 2: Earth's Oceans

Berill, N.J., and Jacquelyn Berrill. *1001 Questions Answered About the Seashore*. New York: Dover.

Coleridge, Samuel Taylor. *The Rime of the Ancient Mariner*. New York: Dover.

Dejong, Meindert. *The Wheel on the School*. New York: Harper & Row.

Hemingway, Ernest. *The Old Man and the Sea*. New York: Macmillan.

Heyerdahl, Thor. *Kon-Tiki: Across the Pacific by Raft*. New York: Washington Square Press.

McClane, A.J. *McClane's North American Fish Cookery*. New York: Henry Holt.

O'Dell, Scott. *The Black Pearl*. Boston, MA: Houghton Mifflin.

Peck, Richard. *Those Summer Girls I Never Met*. New York: Delacorte Press.

Verne, Jules. *Twenty Thousand Leagues Under the Sea*. New York: New American Library.

Wade, Wyn Craig. *The Titanic*. London, England: Penguin.

Chapter 3: Earth's Fresh Water

Garden, Nancy. *Peace, O River*. New York: Farrar, Straus & Giroux.

Grahame, Kenneth. *The Wind in the Willows*. New York: Macmillan.

Moorehead, Alan. *The White Nile*. New York: Harper & Row.

Moorehead, Alan. *The Blue Nile*. New York: Harper & Row.

Pringle, Laurence. *Water: The Next Great Resource Battle*. New York: Macmillan.

Thomas, Charles B. *Water Gardens for Plants and Fish*. Neptune, NJ: TFH Publications.

Twain, Mark. *Life on the Mississippi*. New York: Harper & Row.

Walton, Izaak. *The Compleat Angler*. London, England: Penguin.

Chapter 4: Earth's Landmasses

Adams, Ansel. *Photographs of the Southwest*. New York: New York Graphic Society.

Lasky, Kathryn. *Beyond the Divide*. New York: Dell.

Parkman, Francis. *Oregon Trail*. New York: Airmont.

Riffel, Paul. *Reading Maps*. Northbrook, IL: Hubbard Science.

Rugoff, Milton. *Marco Polo's Adventures in China*. New York: Harper & Row.

Seredy, Kate. *The White Stag*. New York: Viking.

Twain, Mark. *Roughing It*. New York: Airmont.

Chapter 5: Earth's Interior

Asimov, Isaac. *How Did We Find Out About Oil?* New York: Walker.

Goor, Ron, and Nancy Goor. *Exploring a Roman Ghost Town*. New York: Harper & Row Junior Books.

Jackson, Julia. *Treasures From the Earth's Crust*. Hillside, NJ: Enslow.

Lauber, Patricia. *Volcano: The Eruption and Healing of Mount St. Helens*. New York: Bradbury.

Rossbocker, Lisa A. *Recent Revolutions in Geology*. New York: Watts.

Traven, B. *The Treasure of the Sierra Madre*. New York: Farrar, Straus & Giroux.

Wilder, Laura. *West from Home: Letters of Laura Ingalls Wilder*. New York: Harper & Row Junior Books.

Activity Bank

Welcome to the Activity Bank! This is an exciting and enjoyable part of your science textbook. By using the Activity Bank you will have the chance to make a variety of interesting and different observations about science. The best thing about the Activity Bank is that you and your classmates will become the detectives, and as with any investigation you will have to sort through information to find the truth. There will be many twists and turns along the way, some surprises and disappointments too. So always remember to keep an open mind, ask lots of questions, and have fun learning about science.

A MODEL OF ACID RAIN

In many parts of the country, rain contains chemical pollutants that produce harmful effects. You may have read about acid rain. Acid rain can kill fishes in lakes and damage the leaves of trees. In cities, acid rain can damage statues and buildings. You can make a model of acid rain and observe some of the harmful effects acid rain produces.

Materials

3 saucers
3 pennies
vinegar
teaspoon

Procedure

1. Place one penny in each of the three saucers.
2. Place two teaspoons of water on the penny in the first saucer.
3. Place two teaspoons of vinegar on the penny in the second saucer. Leave the third penny alone.

4. Set the three saucers aside and observe the three pennies the next day. (You may want to cover the saucers with a piece of plastic wrap to keep the liquids from evaporating.)

Observations

Describe the appearance of the three pennies. You may want to draw a picture of each penny.

Analysis and Conclusions

1. Explain the changes that occurred in the appearance of the three pennies.
2. What do you think happens to rocks and other objects that are exposed to acid rain over a period of time?

Going Further

With your classmates, see if you can devise a plan to protect the pennies from acid rain. Assume that you cannot stop acid rain from occurring. Present your ideas to your teacher before you test them out.

SINK OR SWIM—IS IT EASIER TO FLOAT IN COLD WATER OR HOT?

Can you float? You may already know that it is easier to float in salt water than in fresh water. Salt water is denser than fresh water. Is it easier to float in warm water or cold? Try this investigation to find out.

Materials

large, deep pan
cold tap water
hot tap water
food coloring
dropper bottle

Procedure

1. Fill a large pan three-quarters full of cold water.

2. Put a few drops of food coloring in a dropper bottle and fill the bottle with hot tap water. **CAUTION:** *Be careful not to scald yourself. The hot water from some taps is very hot indeed!*

3. Place your finger over the opening of the dropper bottle. Carefully place the bottle on its side in the pan of cold water. The dropper bottle should be submerged completely.

4. Slowly take your finger off the opening of the bottle. Observe what happens.

Observations

1. Describe what happened to the hot water.

2. Why did you add food coloring to the hot water?

Analysis and Conclusions

1. Which water, cold or hot, was more dense? Why?

2. Which water, cold or hot, would be easier to float in? Why?

Going Further

Suppose you had placed cold water and food coloring in the dropper bottle and hot water in the pan. What do you think would have happened when you removed your finger from the dropper bottle? With your teacher's permission, test your hypothesis.

Food coloring

HOW DOES A FISH MOVE?

Fishes are well adapted for life in water. In this activity you will observe a fish and discover for yourself how fishes are suited to live in water.

Materials

small goldfish
aquarium
fish food
thermometer

watch or clock
several sheets of
unlined paper

Procedure 🐭

1. On a sheet of unlined paper, draw an outline of the fish from the side. On the same sheet of paper, draw an outline of the fish as seen head-on. On the same sheet of paper, draw an outline of the fish as seen from the top.

2. As you observe your fish, draw its fins on your outlines. Use arrows to show how each fin moves. If a fin doesn't appear to move, indicate this on your drawing.

3. Feed the fish. Record its reaction to food.

4. Take the temperature of the water. Enter the temperature reading in a data table similar to the one shown here. Now count the number of times the fish opens and closes its gills in 1 minute. (The gills are located at the front end

of the fish just behind its eyes. In order to live, fish take oxygen from the water. They swallow water through their mouth and pass it out through their gills.)

5. Add a little warm water to the aquarium. You want to raise the temperature of the water only a few degrees, so be careful. Do not make too drastic a change in the water temperature. Count the number of times the gills open and close in the warmer water in 1 minute.

Observations

1. What fin or fins move the fish forward in the water?

2. What fins help the fish turn from side to side?

3. How does the movement of the gills relate to the temperature of the water?

DATA TABLE

	Gills open and close
Temperature 1	
Temperature 2	

Analysis and Conclusions

What special structures and behaviors enable fishes to survive in a water world?

Going Further

You might like to set up an aquarium that reflects a fish's natural environment more accurately. For example, add a gravel layer to the bottom of the aquarium. Place some rocks and plants in the aquarium. You should then examine your fish's behavior after you have completed this task. What changes, if any, do you note?

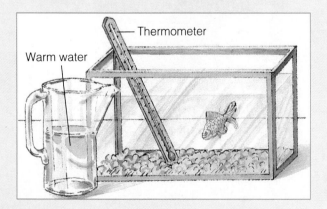
Thermometer
Warm water

Activity Bank

WHAT IS THE EFFECT OF PHOSPHATES ON PLANT GROWTH?

Sometimes seemingly harmless chemicals have effects that are not easily predictable. For example, detergents are often added to water to clean clothes and dishes. When the clothes and dishes are rinsed, the detergents in waste water enter home septic systems or town sewage systems. Detergents in water may eventually be carried to streams, lakes, and sources of groundwater. So far this story seems unremarkable.

However, some detergents contain phosphates. Because of their effects on plant growth, detergents that contain phosphates have been banned by some communities. In this investigation you will measure the effects of phosphates on plant growth. You will uncover reasons why communities try to keep phosphates out of water supplies, and thus ban the use of certain detergents used to clean clothes and dishes.

Materials

2 large test tubes with corks or stoppers to fit

test-tube rack, or large plastic jar or beaker

2 sprigs of *Elodea*

detergent that contains phosphates

sunlight or a lamp

small scissors

Before You Begin

Make sure that the detergent you will be using contains phosphates; many do not. *Elodea* is a common water plant used in home aquariums. A local pet store is a good source of supply.

Procedure

1. Take two sprigs of *Elodea* and use your scissors to cut them to the same length. Measure the length of the sprigs and record the length in a data table similar to the one shown on the next page. Place a sprig of *Elodea* into each test tube.

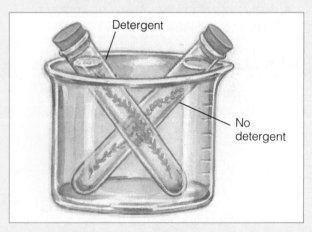

Detergent

No detergent

2. Add enough water to each test tube to fill it nearly to the top. Be sure the *Elodea* sprig is covered with water.

3. Place a small pinch of detergent into one test tube. Gently swirl the test tube to mix the water and detergent. Leave plain water in the other test tube.

4. Stopper each test tube.

5. Place the test tubes in a test-tube rack or plastic jar or beaker. Place the rack (or jar or beaker) in a sunny window or under another source of light.

(continued)

6. Every three days for a month, carefully remove each *Elodea* sprig and measure it. Record your measurements in your data table. Place the sprigs back into the test tubes they were removed from each time. Do not mix up the sprigs!

Observations

1. What was the control in this experiment? Why?

2. Describe the *Elodea* that was placed in plain water.

3. Describe the *Elodea* that was placed in water that contained the detergent drops.

4. Why was it important to return each sprig to the correct tube?

Analysis and Conclusions

1. Did the detergent affect the *Elodea's* growth?

2. How do you explain the results of this investigation?

3. How might the effect of phosphates on water plants affect a community's water supply?

Going Further

Design an investigatation that compares the effects of detergents and fertilizers on plant growth. Have your teacher check the design of your investigation before you begin.

DATA TABLE

	Day	Detergent	No Detergent
	1		
	4		
	7		
	10		
	13		
	16		
	19		
	22		
	25		
	28		
	31		

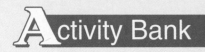
MAKING SOIL

Soil is a substance that is certainly taken for granted by most people. This common substance, often underfoot and easy to see, contributes greatly to human survival. Plants need soil to grow well—it is good, fertile soil that makes our croplands so productive. In this activity you will "make" some soil. Keep in mind, however, that what you can accomplish in an afternoon takes nature's forces many years to produce.

Materials

rocks
sand
magnifying glass
dried leaves

plastic pan or bucket
soil sample

Procedure

1. Use the magnifying glass to examine the rocks and the sand. Draw what you observe on a separate sheet of paper.

2. Place a thick layer of sand in the bottom of the plastic pan or bucket.

3. Break up the dried leaves into tiny pieces. You might even grind the dried leaves between two flat rocks.

4. Add a layer of the ground-up plant material to the sand. Use your hands to gently mix the sand and dried leaves together.

5. Use the magnifying glass to compare the soil mixture you made with the soil sample provided by your teacher. Draw what you observe.

Observations

1. How does the sand compare with the rock samples?

2. Did you observe leaves or other pieces of plant material in the soil sample provided by your teacher?

3. In what ways did the soil you made resemble the soil sample? In what ways was it different?

4. How could you make your soil more like the soil in the sample?

Analysis and Conclusions

1. Where does sand come from in natural soil?

2. Where does the plant material come from in natural soil?

3. Why is plant material an important part of soil?

4. Why are sand and other rock material important parts of soil?

Going Further

Design an experiment to compare the growth of plants in the soil you made with the growth of plants in natural soil. Discuss your plan with your teacher, and get his or her permission before you begin.

HOW HARD IS THAT ROCK?

Hardness is a property that is often used to identify rocks. In this activity you will determine the hardness of several rock samples relative to each other and to several common substances. Geologists often use the Mohs hardness scale to determine the hardness of a rock specimen. But if you are collecting rocks in the field, it may not be easy to carry the ten mineral specimens that represent the Mohs hardness scale along with you. It is often easier to use commonly available substances to perform a hardness test.

For example, a fingernail has a hardness of about 2.5, a penny a hardness of 3.0, a steel knife blade a hardness of about 5.5, and a piece of glass a hardness of 5.5 to 6.0.

Materials

selection of rock samples
square glass plate
steel kitchen knife
penny

Procedure 🔬 📼

1. Select two rock specimens. Try to scratch one with the other. Keep the harder of the two specimens. Put the softer one aside.

2. Select another rock and use the same scratch test. Keep the harder of these two rocks and set the other aside.

3. Keep repeating the procedure until you have identified the hardest rock specimen you have.

4. Compare the rocks to find the second hardest rock. Continue this procedure until all the rock specimens have been put in order from the hardest to the softest.

5. Now compare the rock specimens to the other materials of known hardness to determine the actual hardness of as many of your specimens as possible. **CAUTION:** *Use care when handling sharp materials. Your teacher will show you the proper way to proceed.* Share your results with your classmates. Use their findings to confirm yours.

Observations

1. Did you find any rocks that were softer than your fingernail?
2. Did any rocks scratch the penny?
3. Were any rocks unscratched by the steel blade?
4. Did any rocks scratch the glass plate?

Analysis and Conclusions

1. Calcite has a rating of 3 on the Mohs scale. Would calcite be scratched by a penny?
2. Many people think that diamond (10 on the Mohs scale) is the only mineral that can scratch glass. Is this correct? Why?

Appendix A

The metric system of measurement is used by scientists throughout the world. It is based on units of ten. Each unit is ten times larger or ten times smaller than the next unit. The most commonly used units of the metric system are given below. After you have finished reading about the metric system, try to put it to use. How tall are you in metrics? What is your mass? What is your normal body temperature in degrees Celsius?

Commonly Used Metric Units

Length   The distance from one point to another

meter (m)	A meter is slightly longer than a yard.
	1 meter = 1000 millimeters (mm)
	1 meter = 100 centimeters (cm)
	1000 meters = 1 kilometer (km)

Volume   The amount of space an object takes up

liter (L)	A liter is slightly more than a quart.
	1 liter = 1000 milliliters (mL)

Mass   The amount of matter in an object

gram (g)	A gram has a mass equal to about one paper clip.
	1000 grams = 1 kilogram (kg)

Temperature   The measure of hotness or coldness

degrees Celsius (°C)	0°C = freezing point of water
	100°C = boiling point of water

Metric–English Equivalents

2.54 centimeters (cm) = 1 inch (in.)
1 meter (m) = 39.37 inches (in.)
1 kilometer (km) = 0.62 miles (mi)
1 liter (L) = 1.06 quarts (qt)
250 milliliters (mL) = 1 cup (c)
1 kilogram (kg) = 2.2 pounds (lb)
28.3 grams (g) = 1 ounce (oz)
$°C = 5/9 × (°F − 32)$

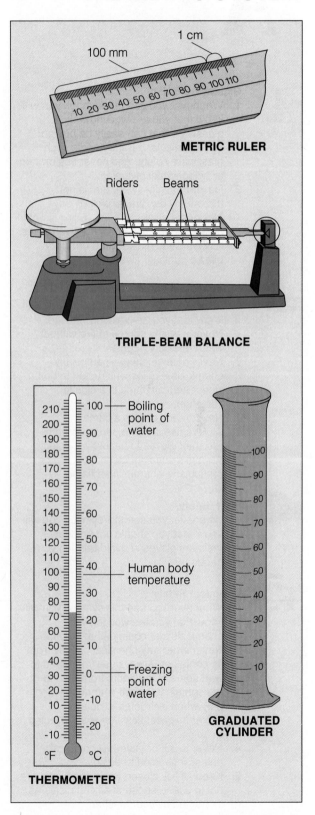

METRIC RULER

Riders   Beams

TRIPLE-BEAM BALANCE

Boiling point of water

Human body temperature

Freezing point of water

THERMOMETER

GRADUATED CYLINDER

Appendix B

Glassware Safety

1. Whenever you see this symbol, you will know that you are working with glassware that can easily be broken. Take particular care to handle such glassware safely. And never use broken or chipped glassware.
2. Never heat glassware that is not thoroughly dry. Never pick up any glassware unless you are sure it is not hot. If it is hot, use heat-resistant gloves.
3. Always clean glassware thoroughly before putting it away.

Fire Safety

1. Whenever you see this symbol, you will know that you are working with fire. Never use any source of fire without wearing safety goggles.
2. Never heat anything—particularly chemicals—unless instructed to do so.
3. Never heat anything in a closed container.
4. Never reach across a flame.
5. Always use a clamp, tongs, or heat-resistant gloves to handle hot objects.
6. Always maintain a clean work area, particularly when using a flame.

Heat Safety

Whenever you see this symbol, you will know that you should put on heat-resistant gloves to avoid burning your hands.

Chemical Safety

1. Whenever you see this symbol, you will know that you are working with chemicals that could be hazardous.
2. Never smell any chemical directly from its container. Always use your hand to waft some of the odors from the top of the container toward your nose—and only when instructed to do so.
3. Never mix chemicals unless instructed to do so.
4. Never touch or taste any chemical unless instructed to do so.
5. Keep all lids closed when chemicals are not in use. Dispose of all chemicals as instructed by your teacher.

6. Immediately rinse with water any chemicals, particularly acids, that get on your skin and clothes. Then notify your teacher.

Eye and Face Safety

1. Whenever you see this symbol, you will know that you are performing an experiment in which you must take precautions to protect your eyes and face by wearing safety goggles.
2. When you are heating a test tube or bottle, always point it away from you and others. Chemicals can splash or boil out of a heated test tube.

Sharp Instrument Safety

1. Whenever you see this symbol, you will know that you are working with a sharp instrument.
2. Always use single-edged razors; double-edged razors are too dangerous.
3. Handle any sharp instrument with extreme care. Never cut any material toward you; always cut away from you.
4. Immediately notify your teacher if your skin is cut.

Electrical Safety

1. Whenever you see this symbol, you will know that you are using electricity in the laboratory.
2. Never use long extension cords to plug in any electrical device. Do not plug too many appliances into one socket or you may overload the socket and cause a fire.
3. Never touch an electrical appliance or outlet with wet hands.

Animal Safety

1. Whenever you see this symbol, you will know that you are working with live animals.
2. Do not cause pain, discomfort, or injury to an animal.
3. Follow your teacher's directions when handling animals. Wash your hands thoroughly after handling animals or their cages.

One of the first things a scientist learns is that working in the laboratory can be an exciting experience. But the laboratory can also be quite dangerous if proper safety rules are not followed at all times. To prepare yourself for a safe year in the laboratory, read over the following safety rules. Then read them a second time. Make sure you understand each rule. If you do not, ask your teacher to explain any rules you are unsure of.

Dress Code

1. Many materials in the laboratory can cause eye injury. To protect yourself from possible injury, wear safety goggles whenever you are working with chemicals, burners, or any substance that might get into your eyes. Never wear contact lenses in the laboratory.

2. Wear a laboratory apron or coat whenever you are working with chemicals or heated substances.

3. Tie back long hair to keep it away from any chemicals, burners and candles, or other laboratory equipment.

4. Remove or tie back any article of clothing or jewelry that can hang down and touch chemicals and flames.

General Safety Rules

5. Read all directions for an experiment several times. Follow the directions exactly as they are written. If you are in doubt about any part of the experiment, ask your teacher for assistance.

6. Never perform activities that are not authorized by your teacher. Obtain permission before "experimenting" on your own.

7. Never handle any equipment unless you have specific permission.

8. Take extreme care not to spill any material in the laboratory. If a spill occurs, immediately ask your teacher about the proper cleanup procedure. Never simply pour chemicals or other substances into the sink or trash container.

9. Never eat in the laboratory.

10. Wash your hands before and after each experiment.

First Aid

11. Immediately report all accidents, no matter how minor, to your teacher.

12. Learn what to do in case of specific accidents, such as getting acid in your eyes or on your skin. (Rinse acids from your body with lots of water.)

13. Become aware of the location of the first-aid kit. But your teacher should administer any required first aid due to injury. Or your teacher may send you to the school nurse or call a physician.

14. Know where and how to report an accident or fire. Find out the location of the fire extinguisher, phone, and fire alarm. Keep a list of important phone numbers—such as the fire department and the school nurse—near the phone. Immediately report any fires to your teacher.

Heating and Fire Safety

15. Again, never use a heat source, such as a candle or burner, without wearing safety goggles.

16. Never heat a chemical you are not instructed to heat. A chemical that is harmless when cool may be dangerous when heated.

17. Maintain a clean work area and keep all materials away from flames.

18. Never reach across a flame.

19. Make sure you know how to light a Bunsen burner. (Your teacher will demonstrate the proper procedure for lighting a burner.) If the flame leaps out of a burner toward you, immediately turn off the gas. Do not touch the burner. It may be hot. And never leave a lighted burner unattended!

20. When heating a test tube or bottle, always point it away from you and others. Chemicals can splash or boil out of a heated test tube.

21. Never heat a liquid in a closed container. The expanding gases produced may blow the container apart, injuring you or others.

22. Before picking up a container that has been heated, first hold the back of your hand near it. If you can feel the heat on the back of your hand, the container may be too hot to handle. Use a clamp or tongs when handling hot containers.

Using Chemicals Safely

23. Never mix chemicals for the "fun of it." You might produce a dangerous, possibly explosive substance.

24. Never touch, taste, or smell a chemical unless you are instructed by your teacher to do so. Many chemicals are poisonous. If you are instructed to note the fumes in an experiment, gently wave your hand over the opening of a container and direct the fumes toward your nose. Do not inhale the fumes directly from the container.

25. Use only those chemicals needed in the activity. Keep all lids closed when a chemical is not being used. Notify your teacher whenever chemicals are spilled.

26. Dispose of all chemicals as instructed by your teacher. To avoid contamination, never return chemicals to their original containers.

27. Be extra careful when working with acids or bases. Pour such chemicals over the sink, not over your workbench.

28. When diluting an acid, pour the acid into water. Never pour water into an acid.

29. Immediately rinse with water any acids that get on your skin or clothing. Then notify your teacher of any acid spill.

Using Glassware Safely

30. Never force glass tubing into a rubber stopper. A turning motion and lubricant will be helpful when inserting glass tubing into rubber stoppers or rubber tubing. Your teacher will demonstrate the proper way to insert glass tubing.

31. Never heat glassware that is not thoroughly dry. Use a wire screen to protect glassware from any flame.

32. Keep in mind that hot glassware will not appear hot. Never pick up glassware without first checking to see if it is hot. See #22.

33. If you are instructed to cut glass tubing, fire-polish the ends immediately to remove sharp edges.

34. Never use broken or chipped glassware. If glassware breaks, notify your teacher and dispose of the glassware in the proper trash container.

35. Never eat or drink from laboratory glassware. Thoroughly clean glassware before putting it away.

Using Sharp Instruments

36. Handle scalpels or razor blades with extreme care. Never cut material toward you; cut away from you.

37. Immediately notify your teacher if you cut your skin when working in the laboratory.

Animal Safety

38. No experiments that will cause pain, discomfort, or harm to mammals, birds, reptiles, fishes, and amphibians should be done in the classroom or at home.

39. Animals should be handled only if necessary. If an animal is excited or frightened, pregnant, feeding, or with its young, special handling is required.

40. Your teacher will instruct you as to how to handle each animal species that may be brought into the classroom.

41. Clean your hands thoroughly after handling animals or the cage containing animals.

End-of-Experiment Rules

42. After an experiment has been completed, clean up your work area and return all equipment to its proper place.

43. Wash your hands after every experiment.

44. Turn off all burners before leaving the laboratory. Check that the gas line leading to the burner is off as well.

MAP SYMBOLS

Boundaries

National . . . .

State or territorial . . . .

County or equivalent . . . .

Civil township or equivalent . . . .

Incorporated city or equivalent . . . . .

Park, reservation, or monument . . . . .

Small park . . . .

Roads and related features

Primary highway . . . .

Secondary highway . . . .

Light-duty road . . . .

Unimproved road . . . .

Trail . . . .

Dual highway . . . .

Dual highway with median strip . . . . .

Bridge . . . .

Tunnel . . . .

Buildings and related features

Dwelling or place of employment: small;

large . . . .

School; house of worship . . . .

Barn, warehouse, etc.: small; large . . . .

Airport . . . .

Campground; picnic area . . . .

Cemetery: small; large . . . .

Railroads and related features

Standard-gauge single track; station . . .

Standard-gauge multiple track . . . .

Contours

Intermediate . . . .

Index . . . .

Supplementary . . . .

Depression . . . .

Cut; fill . . . .

Surface features

Levee . . . .

Sand or mud areas, dunes, or shifting

sand . . . .

Gravel beach or glacial moraine . . . .

Vegetation

Woods . . . .

Scrub . . . .

Orchard . . . .

Vineyard . . . .

Marine shoreline

Approximate mean high water . . . .

Indefinite or unsurveyed . . . .

Coastal features

Foreshore flat . . . .

Rock or coral reef . . . .

Rock, bare or awash . . . .

Breakwater, pier, jetty, or wharf . . . .

Seawall . . . .

Rivers, lakes, and canals

Perennial stream . . . .

Perennial river . . . .

Small falls; small rapids . . . .

Large falls; large rapids . . . .

Dry lake . . . .

Narrow wash . . . .

Wide wash . . . .

Water well; spring or seep . . . .

Submerged areas and bogs

Marsh or swamp . . . .

Submerged marsh or swamp . . . .

Wooded marsh or swamp . . . .

Land subject to inundation . . . .

Elevations

Spot and elevation . . . .   X₂₁₂

Glossary

abyssal (uh-BIHS-uhl) **plain:** large flat area on the ocean floor

abyssal zone: open-ocean zone that extends to an average depth of 6000 meters

air pressure: push on the Earth's surface caused by the force of gravity pulling on the layers of air surrounding the Earth

aquifer (AK-wuh-fuhr): layer of rock or sediment that allows ground water to pass freely

asthenosphere (az-THEEN-oh-sfeer): layer of the Earth directly beneath the lithosphere

atmosphere (AT-muhs-feer): envelope of gases that surrounds the Earth

atoll: ring of coral reefs surrounding an island that has been worn away and has sunk beneath the surface of the ocean

barrier reef: coral reef separated from the shore of an island by an area of shallow water called a lagoon

bathyal (BATH-ee-uhl) **zone:** open-ocean zone that begins at a continental slope and extends down about 2000 meters

benthos (BEHN-thahs): organisms that live on the ocean floor

cavern (KAV-uhrn): underground passage formed when limestone is dissolved by carbonic acid in ground water

coastal plain: low, flat area along a coast (place where the land meets the ocean)

condensation (kahn-duhn-SAY-shuhn): process by which water vapor changes back into a liquid; second step of the water cycle

continent: major landmass that measures millions of square kilometers and rises a considerable distance above sea level

continental glacier: thick sheet of snow and ice that builds up in polar regions of the Earth; also called polar ice sheet

continental margin: area where the underwater edge of a continent meets the ocean floor

continental rise: part of a continental margin that separates a continental slope from the ocean floor

continental shelf: relatively flat part of a continental margin that is covered by shallow ocean water

continental slope: part of the continental margin at the edge of a continental shelf where the ocean floor plunges steeply 4 to 5 kilometers

contour line: line that passes through all points on a map that have the same elevation

convection (kuhn-VEHK-shuhn) **current:** movement of air caused by cool, dense air sinking and warm, less dense air rising

coral reef: large mass of limestone rocks surrounding a volcanic island in tropical waters near a continental shelf

crest: highest point of a wave

crust: thin, outermost layer of the Earth

deep current: ocean current caused mainly by differences in the density of water deep in the ocean

deep zone: area of extremely cold ocean water below the thermocline

elevation: height above sea level

equal-area projection: projection in which area is shown correctly, but shapes are distorted

equator: imaginary line around the Earth that divides the Earth into two hemispheres; parallel located halfway between the North and South Poles

evaporation (ih-vap-uh-RAY-shuhn): process by which energy from the sun causes water on the surface of the Earth to change to water vapor, the gas phase of water; first step of the water cycle

exosphere (EHKS-oh-sfeer): upper part of the thermosphere that extends from about 550 kilometers above the Earth's surface for thousands of kilometers

fringing reef: coral reef that touches the shoreline of a volcanic island

glacier: huge mass of moving ice and snow

globe: spherical, or round, model of the Earth

groundwater: water that soaks into the ground and remains in the ground

guyot (gee-OH): flat-topped seamount

hard water: water that contains large amounts of dissolved minerals, especially calcium and magnesium

hemisphere: northern or southern half of the Earth

hydrosphere: part of the Earth's surface consisting of water

iceberg: large chunk of ice that breaks off from a continental glacier at the edge of the sea and drifts into the sea

impermeable: term used to describe material through which water cannot move quickly; opposite of permeable

inner core: solid, innermost layer of the Earth's core

interior plain: low, flat area found inland on a continent; somewhat higher above sea level than a coastal plain

international date line: line located along the 180th meridian; when the line is crossed going west, one day is added; when it is crossed going east, one day is subtracted

intertidal zone: region that lies between the low- and high-tide lines

ion: electrically charged particle

ionosphere (igh-AHN-uh-sfeer): lower part of the thermosphere that extends from 80 kilometers to 550 kilometers above the Earth's surface

island: small landmass completely surrounded by water

jet stream: strong, eastward wind that blows horizontally around the Earth

landscape: physical features of the Earth's surface found in an area

latitude: measure of distance north and south of the equator

lithosphere: part of the Earth's surface covered by land; solid, topmost part of the Earth

longitude: measure of distance east and west of the prime meridian

magnetosphere (mag-NEET-oh-sfeer): area around the Earth that extends beyond the atmosphere, in which the Earth's magnetic force operates

mantle: layer of the Earth directly above the outer core

map: drawing of the Earth, or a part of the Earth, on a flat surface

Mercator projection: projection used for navigation in which the correct shape of coastlines is shown, but the sizes of land and water areas far from the equator become distorted

meridian (muh-RIHD-ee-uhn): line that runs between the points on a globe or map which represent the geographic North and South Poles of the Earth

mesosphere (MEHS-oh-sfeer): layer of the Earth's atmosphere that extends from about 50 kilometers to about 80 kilometers above the Earth's surface

midocean ridge: mountain range located under the ocean

Moho: boundary between the Earth's outermost layer (crust) and the mantle

mountain: natural landform that reaches high elevations with a narrow summit, or top, and steep slopes, or sides

mountain belt: large group of mountains including mountain ranges and mountain systems

mountain range: roughly parallel series of mountains that have the same general shape and structure

mountain system: group of mountain ranges in one area

nekton (NEHK-ton): forms of ocean life that swim

neritic (nuh-RIHT-ihk) **zone:** area that extends from the low-tide line to the edge of a continental shelf

oceanographer (oh-shuhn-NAHG-ruh-fuhr): scientist who studies the ocean

outer core: second layer of the Earth surrounding the inner core

ozone: gas in the Earth's atmosphere formed when three atoms of oxygen combine

parallel: line going from east to west across a map or globe that crosses a meridian at right angles

permeable (PER-mee-uh-buhl): term used to describe material through which water can move quickly

plain: flat land area that does not rise far above sea level

plankton (PLANGK-tuhn): animals and plants that float at or near the surface of the ocean

plasticity (plas-TIHS-uh-tee): ability of a solid to flow, or change shape

plateau: broad, flat area of land that rises more than 600 meters above sea level

polarity (poh-LAR-uh-tee): property of a molecule with oppositely charged ends

pore space: space between particles of soil

precipitation (prih-sihp-uh-TAY-shuhn): process by which water returns to the Earth in the form of rain, snow, sleet, or hail; third step of the water cycle

prime meridian: meridian that runs through Greenwich, England

projection: representation of a three-dimensional object on a flat surface

relief: difference in a region's elevations

reservoir (REHZ-uhr-vwahr): artificial lake used as a source of fresh water

salinity (suh-LIHN-uh-tee): term used to describe the amount of dissolved salts in ocean water

scale: used to compare distances on a map or globe with actual distances on the Earth's surface

seamount: underwater volcanic mountain on the ocean floor

seismic (SIGHZ-mihk) **wave:** shock wave produced by earthquakes that travels through the Earth

seismograph (SIGHZ-muh-grahf): instrument used to detect and record P waves and S waves produced by earthquakes

shoreline: boundary where the land and the ocean meet

soft water: water that does not contain minerals

solution: substance that contains two or more substances mixed on the molecular level

solvent (SAHL-vuhnt): substance in which another substance dissolves

stratosphere (STRAT-uh-sfeer): layer of the Earth's atmosphere that extends from the tropopause to an altitude of about 50 kilometers

submarine canyon: deep, V-shaped valley cut in the rock through a continental shelf and slope

surface current: ocean current caused mainly by wind patterns

surface runoff: water that enters a river or stream after a heavy rain or during a spring thaw of snow or ice

surface zone: zone where ocean water is mixed by waves and currents

thermocline (THER-muh-klighn): zone in which the temperature of ocean water drops rapidly

thermosphere (THER-moh-sfeer): layer of the Earth's atmosphere that begins at a height of about 80 kilometers and has no well-defined upper limit

time zone: longitudinal belt of the Earth in which all areas have the same local time

topographic map: map that shows the different shapes and sizes of a land surface

topography (tuh-PAHG-ruh-fee): shape of the Earth's surface

trench: long, narrow crevice, or crack, along the edge of the ocean floor

troposphere (TRO-poh-sfeer): layer of the atmosphere closest to the Earth

trough (TRAWF): lowest point of a wave

tsunami (tsoo-NAH-mee): ocean wave caused by an earthquake

turbidity (ter-BIHD-uh-tee) **current:** flow of ocean water that carries large amounts of sediments

upwelling: rising of deep, cold currents to the ocean surface

valley glacier: long, narrow glacier that moves downhill between the steep sides of a mountain valley

Van Allen radiation belts: layers of high radiation around the Earth, in which charged particles are trapped

water cycle: continuous movement of water from the oceans and freshwater sources to the air and land and finally back to the oceans; also called the hydrologic cycle

water table: surface between the zone of saturation and the zone of aeration that marks the level below which the ground is saturated, or soaked with water

watershed: land area in which surface runoff drains into a river or a system of rivers and streams

wavelength: horizontal distance between two consecutive crests or two consecutive troughs

zone of aeration (ehr-AY-shuhn): relatively dry underground region in which the pores are filled mostly with air

zone of saturation (sach-uh-RAY-shuhn): underground region in which all the pores are filled with water

Index